Hill Walkers Donegal

David Herman

Layout by: Declan Moroney
Printed by: Colour Books Ltd., Dublin 13
Sketches by: Ruth Herman
Published by: Shanksmare Publications, 41 Meadow Grove,
  Dublin 16

First Published March 1995

Map based on Ordnance Survey by permission of the Government
(Permit No. 6011).

ISBN 0 9514547 3 0

Cover photograph: Slieve League cliffs

The Author

*David Herman has many years experience exploring the mountains of
Ireland and further afield. Apart from two books covering the Irish mountains in general, he has also written detailed guides to the Wicklow mountains and the hills of Sligo and Leitrim.*

Acknowledgements

*I would like to thank Gaye Moynihan of Donegal County Council and Dr
Kieran O'Keeffe of Glenveagh National Park for help and advice; Goretti
and Malachy Sweeney of Donegal town and John Friel of Creeslough for
their friendliness and hospitality; Paul Hudson for providing the slide
which forms the cover photograph.*

*Lastly and primarily, I once again thank my wife, Mairin Geraty, for
dealing efficiently with all domestic problems and for following me into
terrain where a lesser or less trusting woman would have prudently opted
out.*

Hill Walkers Donegal

34 Sea-cliff and Hill Routes for the Stroller and Mountaineer

David Herman

SHANKSMARE PUBLICATIONS

"In the mountains you forget to count the days"
— *Chinese proverb*

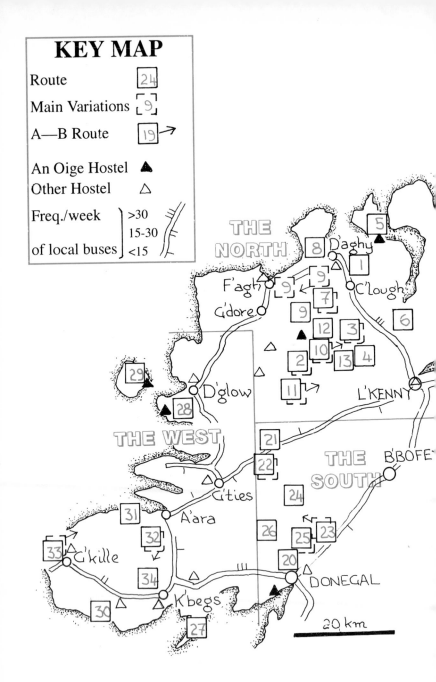

Contents

*Routes with variations

A QUICK LOOK AROUND

Welcome to the county of Donegal, an excellent area for hill walking, since it encompasses challenging peaks, wild and remote uplands, rocky mountain terrain and marvellous sea-cliffs.

Leaving the details for later, I will describe the four main hill walking areas in broad outline, each of these areas corresponding to a section in the book and each described in more detail in the introduction to that section.

The *North* is dominated by three bare, rocky lines of mountains, called collectively the Highlands. Of these three, the northern is graced by probably the most easily recognised mountain in Ireland, Errigal (751m) and the middle by Slieve Snaght (683m). Some of this area is in Glenveagh National Park. North of the Highlands are rugged peninsulas offering good coastal walking.

East of the Highlands is the large peninsula of *Inishowen*, in which the characteristic orientation of the Highlands is faintly continued. Here there is a tiny rocky line of mountains and, in the centre of the peninsula, bulky but unimpressive rolling uplands rising to 615m. There is also plenty of good coastal walking.

The principal mountains of the *South* are a small knot of undulating uplands, the Blue Stacks, which rise to 674m. The central Blue Stacks is a fascinating area of bare rocky knolls, while the rest is grassy and more mundane. As well as the Blue Stacks proper, the hills in the immediate area are included in this section.

Lastly, the *West*, that is the western coastal strip and the bulge of upland sometimes called Rossaun. It hardly needs to be said that this is an excellent area for cliff-top walks, of which the best known is that at Slieve League (595m). Inland, there are good walking areas, though you need to be a little discriminating, as the uplands in places degenerate into bleak moorland.

HOW TO USE THIS BOOK

First of all, it is only fair to state that a map is needed in order to walk most of the routes in this book. More about suitable maps is given below and in each route description.

I have tried to cover all the best and most characteristic of the mountain areas in the county. In doing so, I have taken a 'light and shade' approach, that is I do not describe everywhere and every route as being superlatively good. All routes have some favourable characteristics but some are better than others — in my opinion. Your verdict might well be quite different.

The sketch maps: These accompany nearly all route descriptions and are sufficient for some of the easier walks only. Their aim is to emphasise what is *not* on the maps: cliffs, scree slopes and peat hags. Features which are important for navigation and/or as reassurance points are shown in red. With the exception of the shorter routes, ie. those with a scale line indicating 500m, not 1km, the maps are on a scale of 1:50 000 (that is, the same as the best OS maps).

North is always to the top of the map. The symbols used are explained on the inside back cover.

The *'Walking Time'* given with each route description and the intermediate walking times given at important points on the routes are just that; they do not allow time for rests, photographs or consulting the map. They are based on a walking speed of 4km/hr on the flat and a climbing rate of 500m/hr, so for instance it should take 1½ hours to walk 4km with a climb of 250m. This is not a superhuman rate, but it does reflect mountain terrain where there are few paths and tracks, the situation which pertains over most of Donegal and indeed Ireland. Where the terrain justifies it this walking time is adjusted for difficult terrain (eg steep *descents*, rough vegetation) or easy terrain (eg good tracks).

Metric versus Imperial: At first glance the use of metric and imperial units in this book looks a complete jumble. I have tried to use metric throughout — if you simply can't think metric you can use the tables on the inside back cover — and have used imperial only where necessary. These occasions are two. Firstly where the use of imperial units helps identification of peaks from imperial scale maps (the figures used are cartographically correct, but not necessarily mathematically). Secondly where cars, which are usually equipped with milometers, are involved.

Grid References: These are the four or six digit numbers, preceded by the letters 'GR' which appear in this book after some locations, particularly the start of walks. The figure uniquely identifies the location on most maps. The system is explained on all OS maps.

GETTING TO DONEGAL

BY SEA AND AIR
The nearest ferry ports are at Larne and Belfast, with Dublin/Dun Laoire further away. The nearest international airports are at Belfast, Knock and Dublin.

BY CAR
The main roads into the county are shown on any small-scale road map and it is pointless to laboriously duplicate the information here. In general access is easier from Northern Ireland than from the Republic: there is a motorway (the M1) from Belfast to a little less than half-way to Donegal town. The main roads from the Republic (the N2 from Dublin to North Donegal, the N3 from Dublin to South Donegal and the N15 from Sligo), though of fairly good standard, are far from being motorways.

The N2 and N3 lead into Northern Ireland. At the time of writing the N3 north of Belturbet does not lead directly across the border. Instead you must detour lengthily and slowly using minor roads. It might be worthwhile checking with the AA to obtain up-to-date information.

BY PUBLIC TRANSPORT
There is a frequent Ulsterbus service from Belfast to Derry directly (routes

211 and 212) and to Derry via Strabane (route 273). From Derry there are Swilly Bus services to many towns and villages in north Donegal. (See 'Getting Around Inside Donegal' below.)

The main Bus Eireann express bus services into Donegal are the table 94 (from Dublin to Donegal town via Cavan, about 4 1/4 hours), table 96 (Dublin to Letterkenny via Monaghan, about 4 hours)), table 119 (Galway to Donegal town and Letterkenny, about 5 hrs). This latter service also enables you to travel between the two best local bus termini in the county. Details of all services (express and local) are given in the Bus Eireann timetable (address in the Appendix).

McGeehan's Coaches (phone 075-46101) run a daily service to and from Dublin, with two routes serving towns in south Donegal, terminating in Glencolumbkille and Dunglow. McGinley's Coaches (phone 01-451 3804 or 074-35201) run a daily service to and from Dublin, terminating in Annagary (GR 7919), and on the way serving numerous towns and villages in north Donegal.

There is no rail service into Donegal. The nearest rail heads are at Sligo to the south and Derry to the east.

GETTING AROUND INSIDE DONEGAL

GETTING AROUND BY CAR

The national secondary road with which you will get most familiar is the N56, which follows a circuitous route roughly following the coast from Letterkenny in the north-east to Donegal town in the south. It is of variable quality and the signposting is adequate.

Regional (R-designated) roads are of course not so good and some of the minor roads (unclassified) are almost more pothole than tarmac. The watchword must therefore be: take it easy or you will take it to the garage.

Many minor roads leading to the starting points of walks in this book have no signposting or what is worse, signposting which you cannot rely on. This arises because many finger signposts (ie the ones which are retained on their posts only at one end) are all too frequently either turned to an incorrect position or pointing ambiguously between two roads. It's a nuisance to have to keep one finger glued to the map or half an eye on the milometer but this is preferable to the annoyance caused by getting lost before you even start the walk.

There is another hazard in signposting in or near Irish-speaking areas (or more accurately, supposedly Irish-speaking areas). This is that, in the face of all logic and reason, the signposting is entirely in Irish, though the towns indicated are known to all and sundry by their English versions. In the following panel the Irish language version of towns which you are likely to encounter on signposts in Irish only and which differ significantly from the English version are given.

GETTING AROUND BY REGULAR BUS SERVICE

Two major and several smaller bus companies operate within Donegal. The larger ones are the Swilly Bus Service, which covers the north of the county and the national bus service Bus Eireann, which covers the rest.

The key map (pages 4, 5) gives some idea of the frequency of routes which are of particular interest to walkers. It is valid for outside the summer period, which is narrowly, but perhaps accurately defined as being only July and August (in some cases it's a bit longer). The services are slightly different outside these two months. The services are given for 1994, but do not vary much from year to year.

The bus can be used not only to get you to and from the starting point for looped walks but also, and more imaginatively, to allow linear walks so that you pick up the homeward bus at a different point to your starting point.

A few general points about Bus Eireann and Swilly Bus services:

- It is better value to get a return rather than two single fares, and you can get a return ticket even if you intend to get on the bus for the return at an intermediate point (as would be the case in A to B walks).
- For Bus Eireann services the return fare on Tuesdays, Wednesdays and Thursdays is the same as the single fare.
- Local buses stop anywhere as long as it is safe to do so. Don't expect buses to stop at dangerous corners.
- Express bus fares are the same as local fares.
- Services are generally better on weekdays than on Saturdays and especially Sundays.

Among the towns served by bus the following are near the mountains and so are particularly important for walkers. In this list a figure indicates that the town is served by that Bus Eireann timetable number, Swilly Bus is abbreviated to SB and North-West Busways to NW.

In the North (as defined in this book): Creeslough, Dunfanaghy, Falcarragh, Gweedore (All SB). All these towns are served by a particularly useful service.

In Inishowen: Clonmany (SB, NW), Drumfree (SB), Malin Head (SB).

In the South: Donegal is served by several Bus Eireann routes, with those to Killybegs (299) and Ballybofey (290) being useful for walkers.

In the West: Ardara (298), Carrick (for Slieve League, 296), Glenties (298), Killybegs (296, 298, 299), Glencolumbkille (296), Malinmore (west of Glencolumbkille, 296).

Further information on bus services can be obtained from the addresses in the Appendix. Further details of feasible bus options are given with each route description.

GETTING AROUND BY BICYCLE

Don't forget the humble bike! You can hire bikes in some towns from which the mountains are within striking distance. These towns include (there may be others, especially in the coastal areas) Ardara, Donegal, Falcarragh and Ramelton.

HITCH HIKING

This is an acceptable form of getting around in rural Ireland and it is usually not difficult to get a lift, though if you are soaked to the skin, dripping wet and carrying a large equally wet rucksack your chances will not be enhanced. This is usually the time when you really want a lift! Women travelling alone after dark might be advised to avoid hitching.

ACCOMMODATION

A wide variety of holiday accommodation is available especially along the coast and in the larger towns. Hotel, guest houses and self-catering accommodation is widespread in the county. Details of all these types of accommodation are given in the relevant Bord Failte brochures (address in the Appendix).

If you are specifically on a walking holiday, among the locations you might consider are the string of small towns along the N56 from Creeslough to Gortahork (these towns are suitable for the mountains of the North); Buncrana for Inishowen; Letterkenny (not too far from good walking areas and a hub for the Swilly Bus service); Dunglow, Ardara or Glenties for the West with Glencolumbkille or Killybegs for Rossaun. Donegal town, a good bus centre, is the well placed for the Blue Stacks and some of the mountains to the west eg Slieve League.

There are adventure centres at Gartan Lough in the north and at Malinmore near Glencolumbkille which offer accommodation.

More spartan types might prefer youth hostels or independent hostels.

There are youth hostels at Tra na Rosann on the north coast, at Errigal convenient to the best of the Highland area, on Aran Island and at Crohy Head, both on the remote west coast and at Ball Hill near Donegal town. Note that though there are always self-catering facilities in hostels few will serve meals that are not booked in advance. Details of these types of accommodation are available from An Oige (address in the Appendix).

The Independent Hostel group has hostels in Falcarragh, Glenvar and Dunfanaghy on the north coast; in Doochary and near Crolly (GR 8614) in the Highlands; in Drumfree, Moville and Muff in Inishowen; in Letterkenny and Donegal towns; in Bruckless, Killybegs and Kilcar facing Donegal Bay; and in Glencolumbkille, Dunglow and Glenties on the west coast.

All these hostels are shown on the key map.

MAPS

The mapping of the entire county is excellent. A new series of layer-tinted maps, on a scale of 1:50 000 (about 1 1/4 inches to the mile) with a contour interval of 10m covers the county; the north on sheets 1-3, the centre on sheet 6 and the south on sheets 10 and 11.

Since these are the maps which will be used by most hill walkers it is worth while pointing out a few of their more important characteristics.

- Cliffs are not explicitly depicted, so you must use your judgement by noting the convergence of contour lines. Unfortunately, in the case of some sections of sea-cliff, the contour lines have been omitted altogether, so in these cases you must be careful not to judge absence of contour lines as indicating gentle slopes.
- Far more forest tracks are shown than actually exist. 'Tracks' on the map which ignore the lie of the land and run in straight lines are generally fire-breaks.
- The thin black or grey lines shown in some upland areas are field boundaries of some kind, usually walls or earthbanks.
- Few paths and no footbridges are shown.
- Streams in uplands are badly depicted. You can usually assume that they are narrow and probably fordable in spite of the formidable thickness of the line mostly used.
- It is sometimes difficult to deduce exactly where waterfalls are; they tend not to be shown in remote areas.
- There may not be a trig pillar on the ground where one is indicated on the map, and there may be one where it is not indicated. Discrepancies are noted in the route descriptions.

The alternative to the 1:50 000 series is the old *half-inch to the mile* series which covers the whole county, and much more besides on two sheets, 1 and 3. These maps have a contour interval of 100ft and show cliffs explicitly but not over-accurately. You will get away with using these maps in most areas of Donegal (the notable exception is the Blue Stacks), but the 1:50 000 series is far preferable. For one thing it uses over six times the amount of map paper for each unit area of ground. For another, it is far more up to date. Unless you intend to visit the county for a few days only or are stuck for cash, it is better to invest in the 1:50 000 maps.

If you really are stuck for cash and happen to visit Glenveagh National Park, your luck is in because you get a map free! It covers the National Park and the area around at a scale of one inch to the mile (1:63 360) and a contour interval of 100ft. It shows cliffs explicitly and quite accurately, the only map of the county to do so. At 100ft the contour interval is poor and in damp weather there is the probability of the map falling apart as it is on very flimsy paper.

There is more about suitable maps in each route description.

THE ULSTER WAY (DONEGAL)

There is one long distance path, the Ulster Way (Donegal) which traverses the county roughly from south-east to north-west. It is waymarked, with the exception of the northern section. Since it runs through some remote country it may be difficult to find accommodation everywhere along the route.

The Way starts in Pettigo on the border with Fermanagh, runs by Lough Derg and passes through the Blue Stack mountains where there is a choice of routes. Passing through Fintown, the route crosses some very remote terrain in the Glendowan mountains. From here on the Way is not waymarked. It is intended that it will pass through the Derryveagh mountains to the village of Dunlewy and then run east of Errigal to reach the northern coast at Falcarragh.

SAFETY

Walkers unused to Irish (and British) conditions will be excused if they are asked to read carefully a section on safety, given that they have noted that the highest mountain in the entire county is a puny 750m high.

Do not be misled by such seemingly insignificant heights! Irish mountains in general (and Donegal is no exception) are wild, remote and worthy of respect; it is noteworthy that a high proportion of the fatal accidents in recent years have been suffered by visitors, who did not realise the conditions they were to face.

But let's not be too timid. If you take reasonable precautions and do not try walking in conditions for which you are unprepared, you will enjoy your time in the mountains and return to base safely and with a sense of having achieved something worthwhile.

So, what are 'reasonable precautions'?

- You will get some idea of what to expect on each route from the section on 'Difficulties'. Of course, conditions vary greatly depending on the weather, but you can assume that unless the route is entirely or almost entirely on road, track or path you should wear walking boots.
- The section on 'Difficulties' will also give you an idea of how hard it will be to find your way round the route, but remember that the easiest route to follow in bad visibility is harder than the hardest in good. Cloud and fog make all the difference to navigation. As well as the obvious lack of visibility they are disorienting and distorting, so that what is in reality a minor hill near at hand will appear through cloud like a major mountain much further away. You can get a weather forecast by phoning 1550 123 821.
- Leave word at base of where you intend to go and what time you intend to be back.
- It is definitely prudent not to walk alone and better to have at least four persons. This allows one to stay with the injured if there is an accident and two to try to get help. If the worst comes to the worst, you can summon the mountain rescue services by phoning 999.

WHAT TO CARRY WITH YOU

If you were to carry all the safety equipment that some experts tell you to carry, you would be so weighed down that you wouldn't be able to walk. The most important item to get right are boots, as mentioned in the section 'Safety' above. Apart from that there are only a few things that you really must carry. These include food and a flask with a hot liquid, a whistle and a map and compass. Unless the day looks uncommonly settled and likely to remain so, you should take a waterproof. Lastly, you need a rucksack to put everything else in. Anything else is optional or depends mainly on the weather and the route.

RIGHTS OF WAY

Most of the land over which you walk in Donegal belongs to someone and you are his or her uninvited guest, the major exception being Glenveagh National Park. Landowners are generally trusting folk and will not object to your walking across their land but do not abuse the privilege — and that is what it is. Remember this and behave accordingly.

Specifically:

- Do not bring dogs into sheep rearing country, that is nearly everywhere in the mountains.
- Do not stand on fence wire. It may look the same afterwards but will have been irreparably damaged.
- Leave gates, open or closed, as you found them.
- Do not litter in the mountains — or anywhere else for that matter.
- Exchange a few words with farmers you encounter. It's amazing what you may pick up. For instance, on a recent visit to Glencolumbkille my wife and I met a sheep farmer whose dog pushed stones downhill and then ran after them. Do it yourself stone-throwing for dogs!

THE HIGHEST PEAKS

The following list of the highest peaks in Donegal illustrates the paramount position of Errigal, which is over 70m higher than its neighbour and nearest rival, Slieve Snaght. There is a pleasing variety of locations with high peaks in most areas of the county.

The high points of the Blue Stacks are an anonymous bunch, at least according to the nomenclature of the Ordnance Survey (admittedly some of the Blue Stacks may not even qualify as peaks by some criteria). For the record the local names are 'Blue Stack' for pt 674m, 'Ardnageer' for pt 642m and 'Croaghbann' for pt 641m, thus leaving pt 642m without even a local name.

	Height (m)	Route
Errigal	751	12
Slieve Snaght (Derryveagh)	678	10, 11
Pt 674m (Blue Stacks)	674	24-26
Lavagh More	671	24, 26
Muckish	666	7
Dooish	652	13
Lavagh Beg	650	26
Pt 642m (Blue Stacks)	642	24, 25
Pt 641m (Blue Stacks)	641	24
Pt 626m (Blue Stacks)	626	24, 25
Slieve Snaght (Inishowen)	615	18

The core mountain area of North Donegal is the Highlands, the sternest and wildest area of the whole county. It consists of three long narrow ranges, all of which run in a characteristically south-west to north-east direction. The northern range contains the two very different peaks of Errigal and Muckish, two of the best-known mountains in Ireland, with Errigal at 751m the highest mountain in the county (routes 7, 9, 12). Southwards is the range of bare rock containing Slieve Snaght and Dooish (routes 10, 11, 13) and southwards again the lower and less exciting, remote Glendowan Mountains. Part of these two ranges is in Glenveagh National Park (route 3), the only one in the county. The straight line layout of all three ranges makes looped walks a little difficult but not impossible. The Swilly Bus is therefore useful for A to B routes.

However, the whole of North Donegal does not consist simply of high mountains. Even in the mountain areas easier walks are to be found (routes 2-4, 6), mostly in the vicinity of lakes and usually with excellent views of the higher peaks. In addition, north of the mountain area is a highly indented, rocky, partly cliff-bound coast facing the Atlantic and offering excellent coastal walks (routes 1, 5, 8).

Route 1: ARDS FOREST PARK

Situated between Dunfanaghy (4 miles (6km)) and Creeslough (2 miles (3km)) on the N56, Ards Forest Park has a great variety of scenery and terrain: fenland, lakes, beaches, dunes, rocky faces, deciduous and coniferous trees. It also has a wealth of cultural remains: a dolmen, ring forts. There is a map in the carpark which gives details of the various nature trails and other features. You should easily get a walk of up to 8km or so on the tracks and paths in the park. A small fee is payable at the entrance.

Route 2: DUNLEWY LOUGH

This gives an easy and scenic stroll along the side of a valley and through a pleasant wood. Marvellous mountain views though curiously with little close viewing of the lake circled. If you don't like walking on roads, no matter how scenic, it might be as well to make it a there-and-back walk to the point indicated below.

Getting There: You can start at any point on the R251 which forms much of the circuit. Let's say that you start on the south side of the causeway separating Dunlewy Lough from Lough Nacung Upper (GR 905192). It is reached by passing the youth hostel at Dunlewy on the right, taking the next left and parking on waste ground on the far side of the causeway.

Walking Time: 2 hours (distance 8km, climb 90m) but you will probably

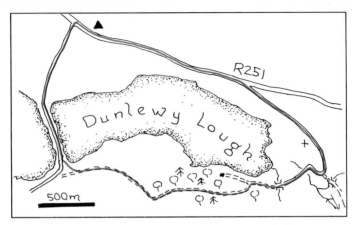

want to take it at a much more leisurely pace than the standard.

Difficulties: Some rough ground to start but otherwise no difficulties.

Map: No map necessary. 1:50 000 sheet 1 shows tracks in the area inaccurately.

Route: Walk initially south-east, so that the lake is on the left, to pick up a track a few metres along. Keep on this track to make an undulating progress over open ground and turn left with it into a wood. At the nearby tee turn right and continue straight ahead on the main track to a tee, with imposing gate pillars off to the left. Turn right at this tee to emerge from the wood onto a road with a pleasant stream on the right and the derelict church further up to the left (0.75 hours). A good place for a rest and from which to return by the same route if you don't fancy a road walk. If you want to go on, take the hairpin bend to pass the church and continue upwards to the R251. Turn left here and of course left again beyond the youth hostel.

Poisoned Glen Variation: While you are in the vicinity it is well worth making the effort to see the Poisoned Glen, surely one of the most memorable (maybe *the* most memorable) easily accessible mountain areas in Ireland. There is more about the Glen under route 10.

Take the track at the hairpin bend just before the derelict church. It leads across a bridge and beyond it follow the stream on the right into the Glen. The end of the Glen is about 2.5km away (about 0.75 hours each way.)

Route 3: GLENVEAGH

An A to B walk, all on track or path, to the Castle which forms the centre point of the National Park, along a straight valley flanked by high hills. Maybe a little too much sameness for those who demand the spice of life. The variation is both quite different and more varied.

Getting There: Let's say you want to get there from the entrance to the National Park. Turn right out of the Park, follow the signs for Church Hill for about 6 miles (10km) to cross the Leannan River (signed). Keep on the main road immediately after the bridge, but then fork next right off it to reach Glendowan. Continue straight ahead for 4 miles (6 km) to a right-angle bend to the left at GR 9715, parking here on waste ground on the right (about 14 miles (23km)) in all.

The non-walking driver should return to the Visitor Centre of the National Park, which is well signposted.

Walking Time: 1.75 hours (distance 8km, no significant climb).

Difficulties: None.

Map: None necessary but take the National Park one-inch map if you have it.

In Glenveagh National Park (route 3)

Route: Cross the gate at the waste ground and start down the track beyond. Keep walking straight ahead! The Castle and Lough Beagh soon come into view in the distance beyond a long straight narrow glacial valley flanked by steep sides, over which pours the occasional spectacular waterfall. When you reach the shores of Lough Beagh you might be a bit disappointed to find that views are mostly concealed by the ubiquitous rhododondron. At the Castle pick up the bus which will take you to the Visitor Centre, where the non-walking driver will have paid the appropriate fee for you into the National Park.

Short There-and-Back Variation: From the Castle (GR 0220) walk around the outbuildings to take the track south-west along the shores of Lough Beagh. Just beyond the lake take what is at first a good track on the left sloping sharply upward. It deteriorates as it climbs and peters out in a high, narrow valley with exceedingly wet ground underfoot. Return by the same route when the ground gets too aqueous (that is, at about the point where it nearly levels.)

Walking time is about 2.5 hours in all but of course it does depend on exactly where you turn back.

Route 4: GARTAN LOUGH

A low level, varied route with practically no climbing, all on track or road around the wooded shores of Gartan Lough. The second half of the walk is mostly by road and might be foregone if time is pressing and a lift is available.

Getting There: Park at Glebe Gallery (1), just off the R251 (at GR 0617). If a lift is available you can arrange to be picked up at Glendowan. To get to Glendowan turn right out of the carpark, go straight ahead to cross the bridge over the River Leannan (signed), fork right immediately to keep on the main road and right again to leave it (signed Colmcille Centre). Drive straight ahead for over 3 miles (5km) to the telephone kiosk on the right (at GR 0213).

Walking Time: 3.25 hours (distance 13km, climb 100m), but if you are picked up at Glendowan this time is roughly halved.

Difficulties: Some wet patches, otherwise easy underfoot.

Map: 1:50 000 sheet 6, half-inch sheet 1 or National Park one-inch map, but none really necessary.

Route: Turn left from the carpark and cross the nearby bridge. Just beyond it, turn left onto a track and simply continue straight ahead for 5km (about 1 hour), there being only one point, after 1.5km or so where you could make a mistake by forking left. The track takes you through a wide variety of scenery: fields, forests, lake and mountain in varied and wondrous combination (2). Beyond the end of the lake take the first turn left to reach Glendowan, where you should turn right for the kiosk or left for the road walk.

The road, which carries a modicum of traffic, is a somewhat inferior version of the outward route. Continue straight ahead where the main road swings right, turn left after 2km from here to pass by the Outdoor Pursuits Centre and the Colmcille Heritage Centre (3), and turn left onto the main road for the Gallery.

Notes

(1) Glebe Gallery contains works by among others Picasso, Kokoschka and Jack Yeats. Beside it is the house of painter Derek Hill, which contains his wide-ranging collection of antiques and art works.

(2) About 2km along the track, on its landward side, are the pitiful remains of some of the houses associated with the Glenveagh evictions of 1861. After the murder of a steward, all 254 of the tenants on the estate were evicted and had to emigrate to Australia.

(3) The Centre gives an interesting history of the life and times of this well-known local saint.

Rocky Cap Mountain (route 10)

RH

Route 5: MELMORE HEAD

Lovely coastal scenery, especially on its western side, with good ever-changing views. The terrain changes rapidly from secluded sandy beaches and grassy slopes to low but impressive sea-cliffs and expanses of rock plunging into the sea.

Getting There: Take the R248 from Carrickart (GR 1336), turn right at the signpost for the youth hostel, pass the viewing area on the right, turn immediately right, turn left at the bottom of the hill and park in Tranarossan carpark (GR 119419) (4 miles (7km) in all). Gallagher's (phone 074-37037) run a regular bus service to the area.

Walking Time: 3 hours (distance 10km, climb about 220m).

Difficulties: None, though you should give yourself plenty of time for negotiating fences (which should be safeguarded) and slippery, treacherous rock.

Map: No map necessary, but take 1:50 000 sheet 2 or half-inch sheet 1 if you have either.

Route: You hardly need any guide to this area. Walk to and along Tranarossan Beach, climb directly north-east to pt 163m/544ft, whose shoulder rises directly from the beach. At the top you will see the whole route and a lot more beside, with Horn Head and Tory Island prominent to the west.

Descend to Boyeeghter Beach (which is not suitable for swimming because of its strong undercurrents) and after that simply continue along the coast to the promontory of Melmore Head, marked by the ruins of a tower (1.75 hours). On the return follow the track and road past several caravan parks to the start. Alternatively (and preferably) keep to the low rocky coast, here punctuated by several sandy beaches, on a longer but more scenic route. At Gortnalughoge Bay head directly for the start.

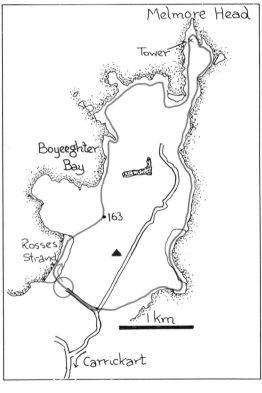

Route 6: LOUGH SALT

Though far from the main mountain centres and surrounded by none too interesting moorland, the tiny upland area centred on Loughsalt Mountain (469m) offers easy walking with excellent wide views.

Getting There: From the north, fork left (signposted) at the shrine in the village of Glen (GR 1130) and continue for 3½ miles (6km) to the carpark on the right. From the south take the N56 north from Kilmacrenan, fork right shortly (signposted), turn left shortly and continue straight ahead to the carpark on the left opposite Lough Salt at GR 1226 (4 miles (6km) in all).

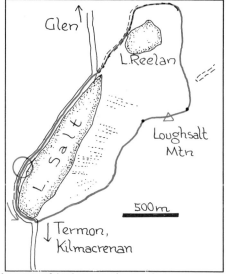

Walking Time: 2.5 hours (distance 7km, climb 360m).

Difficulties: Some high vegetation after Loughsalt Mountain but otherwise fairly good underfoot and easy navigation. Don't be tempted to walk along the seemingly inviting eastern shore of Lough Salt. It's a nightmare of bad vegetation and steep slopes (mostly simultaneously).

Map: 1:50 000 sheet 2, though half-inch sheet 1 should suffice.

Route: From the carpark walk south along the road (ie. keep the lake on the left). Just past the end of the lake, at the ugly pumping station on the left, cross the stile hereabouts and start climbing through high heather. From here on avoid the scree falling to the lakeshore and keep climbing! The three peaks (pts 454m, 469m, about 460m) collectively called Loughsalt Mountain lie within a few hundred metres of one another and will be climbed west to east. The main peak (pt 469m, 1 hour) is easily distinguished by its trig pillar, set amid shattered rocks.

The rest of the route is not over-exciting. From the main peak continue to the east peak and then cross heathery country to reach the northern side of Lough Reelan. Don't descend to the lakeshore; if you keep about 50m above it you will pick up a useful path heading west. This path will take you down through turf cuttings from where a track leads to the road. Turn left here for the start.

Bus Variation: This route or a longer variation might be just about worth doing using the Swilly Bus. Alight at Termon (GR 1122), 4km south of Lough Salt. Take the track beside the church, turn right at the tee and next left. After that it's straight ahead.

Other Variations: The main route is really too short for a full-day walk.

Aided by either map you can lengthen it, though it has to be admitted that there is little out of the mundane in the area around. One route is to continue from Loughsalt Mountain into rolling wet country to the north-east and then head west to reach the north-south tarmaced road between Glen and Lough Salt. Another is to walk tracks through remote country on the western side of Lough Greenan and over Crockmore (GR 1025).

Note

A meteor struck the western side of the mountain in 1821, and for years after the track of scorched heather ending in the lake indicated its route down the hillside.

Route 7: MUCKISH

The great bulk of Muckish (666m), its top a plateau at least a kilometre long and its sides falling everywhere in steep ground, and here and there in scree and cliff, looks from most angles like an upturned ship. The northern approach, the main route given here, should be approached with care in bad weather. Leave time to wander around the summit plateau.

Getting There: From Creeslough take the N56 north (that is towards Dunfanaghy) for over 1½ miles (2 ½km) and turn left just before a graveyard on the right (which is also a good reference point if you are coming in the opposite direction). Drive for 3½ miles (5½ km) to the end of tarmac (GR 005305).

This route might also be walked using the Swilly Bus or a bike.

Walking Time: 3.75 hours (distance 9km, climb 690m).

Difficulties: It is most important to keep to the Miners' Path up the cliffs; there are one or two places where cul de sacs can lead you astray and it is easy to do this in bad weather. There is little to induce vertigo on the path. You may have to do a short diversion on the descent to avoid steep ground. Good underfoot conditions to Muckish summit, after which much soggy ground and some navigation over featureless terrain.

Map: 1:50 000 sheet 2, though half-inch sheet 1 might do in good weather.

Route: Walk onward on the track from the parking place until you reach the old sand loading bays (1), beyond which leftward you will see a steep (nay, well nigh vertical) eroded gully reaching upward to the summit plateau. Well, don't take it (though I believe it is climbable). Instead climb the sandy chute behind the loading bays, cross the narrow stream and pick up the Miners' Path hereabouts (2). This must be followed with care. It consists of a mixture of rough-hewn steps and trodden earth, here and there supplemented by wooden poles. When at length the path crosses a sand-filled gully you can breathe easily again as you are nearly there.

'There' is the quarry from which the quartzite sand used to be extracted. It is a place of some wonder: rusting machinery and crumbling buildings, light-brown rocky pinnacles fronting quarry walls and more than likely the lonely croak of a fluttering raven. Let's move on.

It's only a short climb from here to the summit plateau. If you stand facing out at the quarry edge, the path to the plateau, which is roughly indicated by metal posts, is on your right and winds up over only moderately steep ground. The path peters out near the plateau, but at this point all is simple, with the summit trig pillar (not marked on the 1:50 000 map) close at hand at about GR 005287 (1.75 hours).

As already said, it is worth while taking some time to wander round the summit plateau. The views in all directions are excellent, the northern cliffs magnificent and the terrain, a virtual plateau with one huge cairn in the centre and boulders scattered and heaped everywhere provides easy walking.

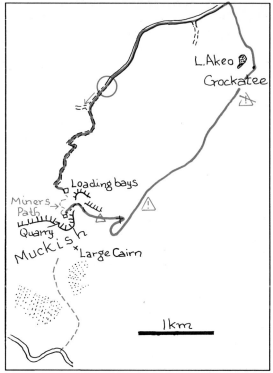

Now for the descent. The steepest feasible point at which to descend eastward is at the white cross about 200m east of the trig pillar. You can make a less steep descent over grass by walking a little clockwise (south-west) from the cross, remembering of course that the further you go south-west the further you will later have to go north-east. The objective on this leg is Crockatee (295m), reached simply by walking north-east, keeping to the high featureless ground.

From Crockatee walk to the high ground to the north of Lough Akeo (shown but not named on the half-inch map), as the lower ground is exceedingly wet. Then, by way of a bog road if you are lucky enough to find it, head directly north-west to tarmac, turn left onto it and walk over 2km to the start.

Easy Variation: It's an easy climb from Muckish Gap to the summit plateau. The Gap (GR 999268) is the highest point on a minor road about 6 miles (10km) south-east of Falcarragh and about the same distance south-west of Creeslough, and is marked by a shrine. From there simply follow the rough path north-east for about 20 minutes, then north-west and north to reach the summit plateau. Take care that you come down at about the same place as there is difficult scree to the west in particular. Walking time is 1 hour to the near edge of the summit plateau.

Notes

(1) Fine quality quartzite sand used in the manufacture of spectacle lens was quarried here until 1955.

(2) Looking back from the Miners' Path you can see the grassy embankments of the Letterkenny and Burtonport Extension Railway. Opened in 1903, it was intended to help the fishing industry in Burtonport. Never a commercial success, it was closed in 1940.

Route 8: HORN HEAD

Marvellous sea-cliff scenery on a peninsula facing Tory Island, with good views landward towards Muckish and Errigal. This is a long but easy walk which can be easily shortened by taking one of the several minor roads which run through the upland centre of the peninsula.

Getting There: From Dunfanaghy take the signposted road for less than a half-mile (1km) to Hornhead Bridge (GR 009375) (1). Park a few hundred metres beyond on waste ground. The Swilly Bus serves Dunfanaghy.

Walking Time: 6 hours (distance 17km, climb about 470m) for the entire walk, including some time for difficult terrain. It is particularly hard to judge total climb in an area where climb can be so easily traded for distance.

Difficulties: Some high vegetation but not normally wet. No navigational problems.

Map: Half-inch sheet 1 or 1:50 000 sheet 2 might be useful if you wish to retreat to the roads in the centre of the peninsula, but not otherwise. If you are using the 1:50 000 sheet note the rather cavalier rendition of contour lines used to depict the cliffs.

Route: The first thing you have to decide is whether to walk anti-clockwise or clockwise, bearing in mind that the more dramatic sea-cliff scenery is on the east. If you think the weather is going to deteriorate (it usually seems to!) walk the route anti-clockwise. As said above you can always retreat to an inland road and since these are closer to the east coast this might be another consideration. I will describe the route briefly in the anti-clockwise direction; the variation below will help you to get started in the opposite direction.

Take the road onward and where it leaves the shore and heads upward, take to the beach. Walk along it for about 1km, at which point a small stream issues into the estuary. Don't attempt to head inland until you are safely past the stream as there is impassable vegetation inland.

After that the route is simple: there are stretches of path which may be some help but the only sure guide is to keep the cliffs, which gradually develop, on the right. The route is generally upward: past Little Horn Head, around a deep amphitheatre sheltering a luxuriant foliage sheltered from the prevailing strong winds, around the shoulder of Croaghnamaddy, until eventually you reach Traghlisk Point and the majestic Horn Head itself, heralded by the ruins of the Signal Tower. Cross a stile at the Head to get a better view of the scene (3 hours) (2).

The return along the somewhat less dramatic west side is equally easily described. Descend south-west and then climb Crockaclogher. As you descend again to walk towards Pollaguill Bay, look back to admire the superb Templebreaga Arch, a 20m high sea arch cut out of the base of Crockaclogher. Pollaguill beach is a good place for a swim, after which short grass and generally good underfoot conditions shorten the stretch to McSwyne's Gun (3).

From the north end of Tramore Strand (the large beach not named on the half-inch map) a spot of compass work may be needed, aiming across the sand dunes to reach the northern side of Hornhead Bridge. Keeping forest on the left you may be lucky enough to pick up a track or path ending at a gate at the bridge. Once on the road turn left for the car or right for Dunfanaghy.

Start of the Clockwise Route: Walk back to Hornhead Bridge, and on the near side cross the gate and follow the path beyond. After about 350m cross a stile and ditch. Then follow a track heading roughly for Tramore Strand. It tends to lose itself so a compass bearing might be useful if you decide the track is not much help.

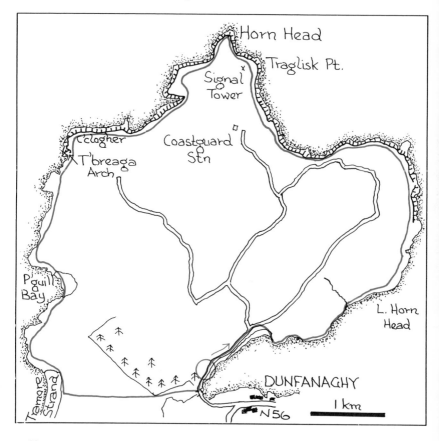

Notes

(1) The Horn Head peninsula was once an island. Sand was blown from the west to form a bridge to what is now the peninsula, as you can see from the sandy terrain between Dunfanaghy and here. Older maps show the lake, now significantly called 'New Lake', as an inlet of the sea open to the west.

(2) A wide range of birds, not all of them sea birds, nest and breed on or near the 190m high cliffs here. They include kittiwakes, guillemots, puffins, peregrines, choughs and ravens.

(3) This cavern is situated just north of the narrow inlet shown on the 1:50 000 map about 400m from the end of Pollaguill Bay. In former times the compressed air forced out of the cavern produced a noise that could be heard miles away when the wind was in the right direction. In recent times however the aperture has widened and the noise is not so impressive.

Route 9: AGHLAS

The three graceful cones of the Aghlas, dominating Lough Feeane, lie between Errigal and Muckish. All three offer excellent views of both peaks, as well as further afield. From the north they form a memorable and what is more a natural circuit, the latter a rarity in this area.

Getting There: From Falcarragh take the road south from the centre of the village, forking left after 0.4 miles (0.6km) and right after another 0.7 miles (1.1km). Fork left uphill after another 2.6 miles (4.2km) and park just past the fish farm gates on waste ground (GR 936258). This point can also be reached from Gortahork.

It's just about feasible to do this walk by using the Swilly Bus, though it's a lengthy 7km from Falcarragh and somewhat less from Gortahork. You might be lucky enough to get a lift part of the way.

Walking Time: 4 hours (distance 9km, climb 700m).

Difficulties: Boggy terrain in the lower ground but otherwise excellent. Easy navigation.

Map: Unfortunately, two 1:50 000 maps (sheets 1 and 2) are needed with consequent lack of cartographic cohesion. In good weather half-inch sheet 1 should suffice.

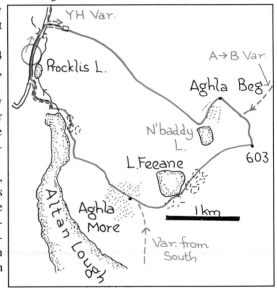

Route: Walk back along the road from the parking place to cross the first bridge. Take the first turn right to a nearby deserted farm and continue beyond it south-east using what tracks you can find to reach the shores of Nabrackbaddy Lough (marked but unnamed on the half-inch map). This initial stretch to the lough is definitely the most boring of the entire route, so you will doubtless be pleased to reach the lake and contemplate the trio of fine peaks which here rise all around.

The first climb is a direct one through occasional patches of scree to the huge cairn on Aghla Beg (564m/1860ft, 1.75 hours) from where the view is magnificent, encompassing a wide range of lovely mountains in nearly all directions.

The second of the Aghlas lies over high easily traversed ground to the south-east and the views on this stretch are just as good as they were from the top of Aghla Beg. This Aghla (603m, over 1900ft) is unnamed on the maps and on the half-inch map is depicted as a plateau (it isn't). In spite of these cartographic denigrations the views from this, the highest of the Aghlas, are just as good as from Aghla Beg.

The descent is through peat hag country towards the large Lough Feeane. From close to the shores of the lake the ascent to Aghla More (584m, 2.75 hours) is obvious, a stiff one at this late juncture.

From the small cairn on Aghla More a little care is needed on the descent to avoid scree on the south-western and northern sides. Walk initially at about 310 degrees compass from the small summit cairn, and after a few hundred metres you can veer right to reach easier ground and eventually the shores of Altan Lough, where slow progress ensues through difficult haggy ground.

Walk to the northern end of Altan Lough where you may cross by fording the river close to the lake or at the stepping stones a little further on (wet feet may result, though at this late stage it should not be too discomforting). Take the track running north along the opposite shore. This ends at a gate; turn right onto the road to reach the nearby parking place.

Variation from the South: Not a good natural circuit and with some dull ground to be traversed (twice!) but convenient if you are staying south of the Aghlas. Start at the Altan Farm pillar on the R251 (GR 952205). Take the track from here to the shores of Altan Lough, climb Aghla More (2 hours), descend to Lough Feeane (remember to start off at 310 degrees compass), walk south of Nabrackbaddy Lough and then follow the main route, descending to Altan Lough after climbing the pt 603m Aghla. Walking time is 5.25 hours (distance 13km, climb 930m).

Youth hostel Variation. If you intend to stay at Errigal youth hostel you can get the Swilly Bus to Falcarragh or Gortahork, climb Aghla More (3.25 hours), descend to the eastern corner of Altan Lough and take the track from there to the R251. This route requires only one 1:50 000 sheet (sheet 1). Walking time from Falcarragh is 5.75 hours (distance 19km, climb 750m).

Muckish Gap to R251 Variation. The central and longest section of the annual Glover Highlander Marathon Walk is exhilarating, with much the same characteristics of the main route above. The maps are as above.

Start at the shrine at Muckish Gap (GR 999269). Keep forest on the left to ascend to the virtual plateau of Crocknalaragagh (pts 461m, 454m) where the small lakes are better landmarks in exceptionally soggy terrain than the nondescript 'peaks'. Descend to the shore of Lough Aluirg and keeping it on the left, cross its outlet stream and climb the spur to the south-west to near the summit of Aghla Beg. Climb Aghla Beg (2.5 hours), Aghla (pt 603m), Aghla More, descend to the eastern corner of Altan Lough. Take the track running from here to reach the R251 at Altan Farm pillar (GR 952205). Walking time is 5 hours (distance 12km, climb 930m).

Route 10: SLIEVE SNAGHT AND THE POISONED GLEN

The quartzite dome of Slieve Snaght dominates the Derryveagh Mountains, whose rocky crest is riven by low crosswise parallel cliffs. These cliffs contribute to making this some of the most difficult — and rewarding — terrain in Donegal. The possible route options are many but this one taking in the Poisoned Glen is probably the best of an excellent selection.

Getting There: Start at the derelict church just south of the R251 in Dunlewy (GR 929190). There is plenty of room to park hereabouts. If you are staying at the youth hostel there is an attractive route to this point (route 2).

Walking Time: 4.75 hours (distance 12km, climb 710m).

Difficulties: Easy underfoot until near the end when much boggy terrain has to be endured. In good visibility no navigational difficulties especially with the huge cone of Errigal across the valley to act as a constant landmark. In bad weather much more difficult on the high ground to Lough Slievesnaght; that lake is a useful landmark (or lakemark?).

Map: 1:50 000 sheet 1 is much preferable to half-inch sheet 1 which fails to show the complexity of the terrain, though in good visibility it will probably do. The area is also quite well depicted on the National Park one-inch sheet, which shows the cliffs of the Poisoned Glen best of all.

Route: From the start you can see most of the route with the great silvery dome of Slieve Snaght prominently rising amidst expanses of bare grey rock. An awe-inspiring sight! Walk down the road from the church to take the track at the nearby hairpin bend. This leads across a bridge and from there you can follow the stream on the right into the Poisoned Glen. As you advance over level, boggy ground the steep grey rocky walls of the Glen close in on the sides and ahead, apparently leaving the inward route as the only escape.

Not so. Keep by the stream to the end of the valley, where it (the stream)

takes a decided right turn in the direction of flow. Cross it here and climb the grassy ramp directly ahead; it is a tough but not vertigo-inducing ascent to the top of the cliffs and to a rocky rib overlooking Lough Atirrive Big (1.5 hours).

The stretch from here to Lough Slievesnaght to the south-west is a difficult one navigationally in bad weather. It consists of an undulating

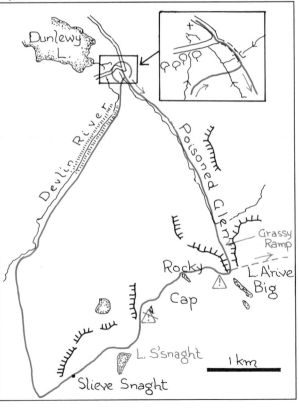

climb over a flattish peak known locally as Rocky Cap (over 580m, 1800ft), followed by a steep descent to the lake, this progress punctuated by a series of low crosswise dykes (1), some of which shelter tiny lakes. After the indeterminate summit of Rocky Cap, your advance to the south-west is abruptly terminated by the north–south cliffs which mark its western end. Some of the slabs of vertical rock around here form rough rectangles (one is cantilevered over the void); these are as good an indication as any of the imminence of the cliffs.

It is best to approach the northern end of Lough Slievesnaght from the north-east where a grassy ramp aids the descent to this large lake, a good setting for a rest. From here it is a straight climb to Slieve Snaght (3 hours), which is crowned by a sturdy cairn and from which the views can scarcely be equalled in Donegal, with Errigal, the Aghlas and Muckish and a whole panorama of mountain and coastline to be enjoyed in all directions.

Descend south-west from Slieve Snaght to avoid cliffs to the west. This will take you to a col from which you can descend north to reach the right bank of the Devlin River. Follow it at a respectable distance because its banks are swampy and because it runs in a deep-set ravine sheltering a thick mass of trees and shrubs which could not grow on the open moorland. If you simply must cool off however there are delightful pools to be found here and there along its route.

As you near the road you will be forced from the Devlin River by a thick wood, so that you will have to ford a stream on the right. To reach the nearby start, you must cross the initial (and only) bridge of the day.

An A to B Variation: Leave one car at the junction at GR 019248, that is 7 miles (12km) north-east along the R251 from the start. Map: Use the National Park one-inch map or half-inch sheet 1 in good weather. The National Park map is particularly useful because it shows cliffs. If you use the 1:50 000 series you will need two sheets (1, 6) and maybe even a tiny section of a third (2).

Follow the main route above to climb the cliffs of the Poisoned Glen (1.5 hours), walk east to cross the deer fence in a tiny cliff-bound valley, continue east for 500m, then swing north to descend to Lough Beg (GR 9518), climb Maumlack (1589ft, 3.5 hours). (Most of the rest of the route is described under route 13.) Walk over Edenadooish to Dooish (5 hours). Continue northeast to Saggartnadooish and pt 391m, climb Kingarrow, cross the deer fence to reach the road junction. Walking time is 6.5 hours (distance 15km, climb 1080m).

Note

(1) These mark the lines of igneous dykes. In a geologically recent era, hot magma was thrust up vertically from the bowels of the earth and pushed aside the existing rock. The cooled magma has proved to be less resistant to erosion and has been worn away quicker than the pre-existing rock, thus leaving the dykes.

Route 11: SLIEVE SNAGHT FROM THE SOUTH

If you are staying south of the Highland area it is more convenient to tackle Slieve Snaght from the R254, which runs south-east of the Derryveagh Range. This approach is not so good as that from the north but in an area where everywhere is little short of superb, this is nonetheless an excellent circuit.

Getting There: The start is about 13 miles (21km) east of Dunglow. Take the N56 towards Glenties, turn left onto the R252, in Doocharry take the R254 for 5 miles (8km) to the carpark on Lough Barra at GR 929124.

Walking Time: 4 hours (distance 9km, climb 640m), including some time for boggy terrain.

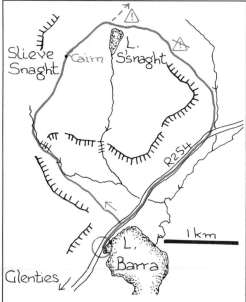

Difficulties: Navigation generally easy except for a short stretch after Lough Slievesnaght. Terrain good in higher ground but very wet lower.

Map: 1:50 000 sheet 1 is much better than half-inch sheet 1, but the latter will suffice in good weather. The area, and especially its cliffs, is also well depicted on the National Park one-inch sheet.

Route: Walk north-east along the road from the carpark, that is onward if you have come from the Dunglow direction, and after a few hundred metres take to the soggy ground to the left, thus rounding a line of cliffs. The idea here is to push north-westwards towards the waterfall at the end of the valley, so do not confuse it with the one that comes into view first and which is on its northern side. This is a very wet stretch and it might be as well to gain some height to avoid the worst of it.

Climb with the waterfall on the right, keeping clear of the long slabs on this (and indeed on the other side) if you feel nervous. At the top of the waterfall you can veer away from the stream above it and climb through boulders to the solid cairn on the top of Slieve Snaght (678m, 2.25 hours).

From Slieve Snaght descend directly to the northern end of Lough Slievesnaght and from here — and this is the only point in the route where the terrain is of no help in route-finding — head directly east for about 600m (say 10-15 minutes) to cross a low ridge. Once in, or at the side of, a soggy valley head south-east to the road, and turn right onto it to reach the parking place about 2 km away.

A to B Variation: It is obvious from the layout of this range that, without a second car, for every kilometre on the mountains you will have to walk one on the R254 which, although remote and scenic is also quite unvarying. With two cars however you can leave one about 2½ miles (4km) further north-east, where there is room for careful parking along the road. (You can of course make an even longer route along the range but if you go much further than suggested here you will have to descend to the deep valley containing Lough Beagh. You will also need 1:50 000 map sheet 6.)

Take the main route to Lough Slievesnaght, climb a grassy ramp to reach the indistinct plateau of Rocky Cap to the north-east, descend to the top of the Poisoned Glen north of Lough Atirrive Big (shown but not named on the half-inch and National Park maps). From here keep to the high ground east of that lake for as long as possible so as to avoid the extremely wet ground in the valley containing the lake. Walking time is 4.25 hours (distance 9km, climb 850m).

Route 12: ERRIGAL

Probably the most recognisable peak in Ireland, Errigal is a graceful, almost perfect quartzite cone, its sides falling in white and grey scree slopes hundreds of metres to undulating moorland. At 751m it is the highest peak in Donegal and so a worthy goal. The only easy approach is from the east side. This gives an easy up and down walk; to make a convincing circuit requires a little more effort.

Getting There: The start, which is about 12 miles (19km) south-west of Creeslough and 15 miles (24km) north-east of Dunglow, is at an intermittent path off the R251 (at GR 947199). This point is 0.5 miles (0.8km) west of the gate pillar for Altan Farm (easily missed!) and 1.6 miles (2.6km) east of the side turn right (as you drive east) signed 'Poisoned Glen'. There are several other places along the road west of the Altan Farm pillar where you can park and which are almost equally good starting points.

If you are staying at Errigal youth hostel and have no transport, the path starting nearly 3km east of the hostel is more convenient, but make sure you find the one and only path through the scree slopes to the summit.

Walking Time: 4.5 hours (distance 8km, climb 680m). An up and down to the summit of Errigal should take about 2.5 hours, but the descent time may vary greatly, as some people can hop quickly down loose rock, while others must take it very slowly.

Difficulties: Some boggy ground before and after the path through scree on Errigal. Navigation is simple on the Errigal section of the route but thereafter more difficult with some scree slopes to avoid.

Map: 1:50 000 sheet 1, though half-inch sheet 1 or the National Park one-inch map will do.

Route: Walk the intermittent path directly uphill over boggy ground, keeping a watch for a set of stout fence posts which marks the start of the path through scree over the eastern spur of the mountain. Once on this path keep to it (easy, as there is no alternative), noting the two cairns on the right of the path marking the point where you must divert to Mackoght if you intend to walk the entire route.

The stony path takes you into a terrain of extensive scree slopes dropping straight from the summit. It's a simple vertigo-free progress; within 5-10 minutes of its end you attain the crest of the ridge where the path is marked by a set of cairns, into one of which is set the Joey Glover memorial (1).

The summit, probably the smallest in Ireland, consists of two tiny peaks about 30m apart, joined by a narrow ridge. It is a superb viewpoint, with the mountain's surrounds seemingly at your feet and much of Donegal and beyond within view. Slieve Snaght, the huge dome to the south, and the great line of hills stretching to Muckish are the most prominent, but on good days you can easily recognise Benbulbin in Sligo.

Retrace your steps from the summit to the two cairns noted earlier and then, with a strange area of small rocky drumlins (2) on the left, follow a rocky ridge directly to Mackoght (555m, over 1600ft). In bad weather this is a difficult summit to find, as it has a few rocky high points, each with a cairn. However what is unmistakable are the steep scree slopes along its northern side. Carefully avoiding these, descend initially east and then climb north to the undistinguished Breaghy (395m, over 1200ft), watching out for the scree slopes on *its* northern side. Breaghy's one attraction is the excellent view it offers over Altan Lough, with the Aghlas towering behind.

From Breaghy descend east to reach a wide and soggy track after less than a kilometre. Turn right onto it to cross moorland and reach the R251, where a right turn will take you to car or hostel.

Longer Variation: From Breaghy it is easy to descend to the castle ruins at Altan Lough and a good deal less easy to climb Aghla More (4.25 hours). Total walking time 6 hours (distance 13km, climb 1340m).

Notes
(1) The Joey Glover Memorial: Though the plaque does not say so, Joey Glover was murdered by the IRA in one of their many 'mistakes'.
(2) These appear to be drumlins, and so formed by the passage of ice. Drumlins however are normally of soil, not stones as these are.

Route 13: DOOISH

At 652m, Dooish is *primus inter pares*, the highest point in the lengthy line of bare and rocky mountains, none of which is particularly dominant, in the section of the Derryveagh Mountains which stretch north-east from Slieve Snaght. The route starts at scenic Lough Beagh, focus of Glenveagh National Park (1), and traverses the Derryveagh Mountains to reach Dooish. The entire route lies within the Park, and a shuttle bus may be used to help form a convincing circuit. There is a good chance of encountering some of the Park's herd of red deer.

Getting There: Before you go there, read note (1) below. The entrance to the Park (GR 0323) is well signposted from all directions. It is about 7 miles (11km) south of Creeslough and about 14 miles (23km) north-west of Letterkenny.

Walking Time: 5.25 hours (distance 15km, climb 750m).

Difficulties: Lots of wet ground. Navigation generally easy though there are long stretches without distinct features. Mistakes are not dangerous but take care around the cliffs and steep ground north-west of Lough Beagh.

Map: 1:50 000 sheet 6 is far preferable to half-inch sheet 1. The National Park one-inch sheet, which you get at the Park entrance, is acceptable.

Route: From the Castle, walk between the outbuildings to reach a clear track which runs for about 3km along the south-east shore of Lough Beagh, though the view of the lake is unfortunately obscured by rhododendron. At the end of the lake cross a footbridge on the right over the Owenveagh River and set your sights on the majestic Astelleen Waterfall close by to the left across the narrow valley.

There is no easy way of reaching the waterfall: the intervening ground is always wet and the tussocks make for hard going. At length, though you may doubt it at the time, you will reach the foot of the waterfall and ford the stream below it. Next climb by the side of the waterfall (informed opinion states that the ascent is easier on this side); you will probably have to veer away from it near the top to avoid rocky crags, though the ascent is not perilous.

At the top of the waterfall you find yourself in a high, bare, gently sloping valley. Follow the stream north-west for about 1.5km, at which point the main stream veers sharply to the right as it descends. Here climb steeply, at last out of soggy country and into more rocky terrain, north-west to Edenadooish (521m, over 1600ft) (2) (on the National Park map this is shown as the south-west spur of Dooish). You might note that in bad weather the high deer fence, whose direction changes by over 90 degrees between the two summits of Edenadooish, is a good landmark.

Turn north-east from Edenadooish to face the stiff climb to Dooish itself, the goal of the route. Crowned by a well-constructed cairn and with cliffs on its northern face, Dooish (652m, 3.25 hours) commands good views especially towards the Errigal-Muckish range, views which are enhanced if you walk towards the cliffs.

Drop steeply from here to Lough Aleahan (just about shown on the half-inch map). You will see from the 1:50 000 map (but not so evidently on the National Park map) that there is a long narrow cleft starting just south-east of the lough and running parallel to the general south-west to north-east trend of the range. (Incidentally in the floor of the cleft is a small rocky mound (pt 360m at GR 003222) which may be a useful landmark in bad weather.) Keeping to the north-west of this cleft, cross the bare rocky erratic-strewn plateau of Saggartnadooish, and continue over similar terrain to climb pt 391m (over 1200ft). From here descend to Misty Lough North and South in turn, both of which snuggle in wet country south of Kingarrow.

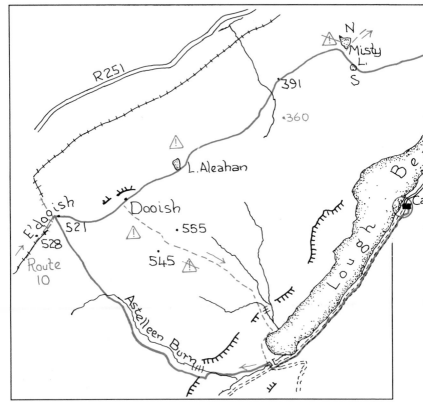

From here to the Visitor Centre the object is to keep as far away from Lough Beagh as possible, as the nearer to the lake you walk the wetter the ground and the higher the tussocks. At length you will reach a gate at the western edge of a mature wood. From here, it is a short stroll by track back to the Centre.

The Shorter Variation (Maybe): If you are tired or find that time is short when you reach Dooish, you might be able to save a little on this variation, but only if you are agile on steep descents. Don't forget that since this variation ends at the Castle you may have to wait for a bus or walk to the Visitor Centre.

Walk south-east from the summit and cross between the two dumpy peaks of its south-east outlier (555m and 545m, over 1700ft). Continue south-east to make a steep descent over grass to the right of a waterfall and so reach the shores of Lough Beagh at about GR 002193. Make sure you find this descent route as there are rocky crags and cliffs on both sides of it. Use the outward route for the return. Walking time is 5 hours (distance 15km, climb 640m).

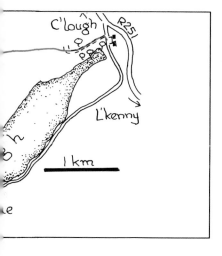

Notes

(1) From September to February inclusive, if you intend to leave tracks and paths you must get permission from the Park authorities (address in the Appendix) as there is likely to be deer culling during this period.

There is a small charge into the Park. Cars must be left at the Visitor Centre (GR 039232). From there the bus, when running, will take you to the Castle (GR 020209) where the route starts. The bus runs only in summer. At other times you face an additional walk of 3.5km.

The Visitor Centre here has a great deal to interest the outdoor person, with an audio-visual display and an exhibition. The Castle and its gardens, a formal space in the midst of wild splendour, is also worth a visit.

(2) Around here you can see the first of the straight line dykes which run across the grain of the mountain range nearly as far as Slieve Snaght. There is more about this under route 10.

A large peninsula flanked by two long inlets to east and west, Inishowen is known as 'Ireland in miniature', though if it is, it is the best of Ireland in miniature. Attractive and neat villages, pleasant wooded areas and a superb coastline make it a good tourist area.

The hills of Inishowen bear the south-west to north-east imprint of the Highlands, though less firmly. The highest point is bulky but mundane Slieve Snaght (615m) (route 18), though the narrow line of hills to its north-west, centred on a steep winding road through the Gap of Mamore (routes 15-17) offers much better walking. There is also much good walking to be had along the rugged, remote, indented coast (routes 14, 19), especially that to the north facing out towards Scotland.

Route 14: DUNAFF HEAD

An easy walk around Dunaff Head, which gives excellent rocky coastal scenery with — and this is unusual for sea-cliff walks — a convincing looped route.

Getting There: Drive to Dunaff village (GR 3247), which is about 12 miles (19km) north of Buncrana. Pass Dunaff post office on the left, turn right at the tee and continue straight ahead to near the end of this road, where there is a side road on the left (GR 324486).

Walking Time: 2 hours (distance 6km, climb about 250m).

Difficulties: Mostly rough but generally dry ground underfoot. No navigational difficulties.

Map: None necessary but take 1:50 000 sheet 3

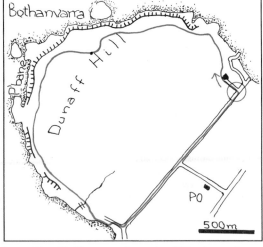

or half-inch sheet 1 if you have either. Neither map shows the cliffs adequately.

Route: Take the side turn and at its end keep the fence on the left to walk through an area lush with a wealth of knee-high flowers and plants of all descriptions. A continuous climb with wicked, vertical cliffs on the right extends as far as the first island, Bothanvarra, after which the ground tends to level and the cliffs assume a more rounded, grassy profile.

At the inlet beyond the grass- and lichen-covered second island, you may decide to walk down towards the sea, here bordered by low cliffs and rocky inlets. If so you might note that you will have to climb about 50m towards the end to surmount a final section of cliff. Past this section, cross a low waterfall issuing directly into the sea and keep fences on the left to reach a small, stony beach. Take the track at this beach to reach tarmac, turn right onto it and left at the nearby tee. Walk straight ahead less than 2km on road to the start.

Tormore (route 33)

Route 15: BULBIN

The bare grassy hill of Bulbin with its rugged rocky ribs to north and south is easily climbed and provides an excellent viewing point in all directions.

Getting There: Cross the Clonmany River out of Clonmany, turn left immediately, keep straight ahead for 0.9 miles (1.5km), turn right uphill here and drive for a further 1.2 miles (2.0km) to park just beyond or at the first turn (at GR 358435) on the left.

This walk may also be easily be done by taking the Swilly or North-West Bus to Clonmany and starting the walk there.

Walking Time: 2 hours (distance 5km, climb 350m).

Difficulties: Some wet ground, otherwise good. Navigation is easy, but beware of the short stretch of cliff on the north side of the summit which is not adequately indicated on the maps.

Map: 1:50 000 sheet 3 or half-inch sheet 1 hardly necessary in good weather.

Route: Walk onward from the start on a road which eventually deteriorates to a stony track and then curves in a gentle arc round the western side of the mountain. When, after about 2km from the start the track levels out amid boggy, higher ground on both sides, it is time to take to trackless country.

So, turn left off the track and climb directly to the summit, a steep rocky slope on the left and the summit memorial increasingly obvious ahead. The summit itself is a good standpoint from which to study the mountains on both sides of the Gap of Mamore westward and the Slieve Snaght area in the south-east, as well as a wealth of coast and other mountains. The memorial itself, built to commemorate the Eucharistic Congress of 1931 has a receptacle claiming to contain holy water. If so, it must attain holiness on its downward passage as secular rain!

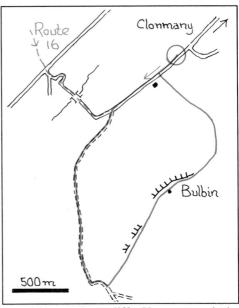

Keeping a wary eye on the cliffs to the left keep onward and downward from the summit, veering left to keep to the high ground when safely past these cliffs. You can reach the 'main' road, on which you started walking, anywhere between the side road and the first house on the near side of the 'main' road. Don't attempt to reach the road to the left of this house as there are young trees there.

Route 16: RAGHTIN MORE

This is the northern end of the narrow line of hills which stretch to the sea at Dunree Head. A walk along a wooded defile is followed by an exceptionally wet stretch through bogland before the higher and drier ground is reached. These uplands are grassier, more rounded and generally less spectacular than the Urris Hills to the south, but nonetheless offer superb views over mountain and coast. The entire range to Dunree Head may be easily walked if transport is available at the end (see the variation below).

Getting There: Cross the Clonmany River out of Clonmany, turn right immediately, and drive for 0.8 miles (1.3km) to park carefully at the bridge at Glen House (GR 359469).

Swilly and North-West Buses serve Clonmany, from where the route may easily be walked.

Walking Time: 4.5 hours (distance 11km, climb 820m).
Difficulties: Much wet ground in the lower, flatter areas. Navigation generally easy though the ascent to the Slievekeeragh ridge is a little indeterminate.
Map: 1:50 000 sheet 3 but half-inch sheet 1 will do.

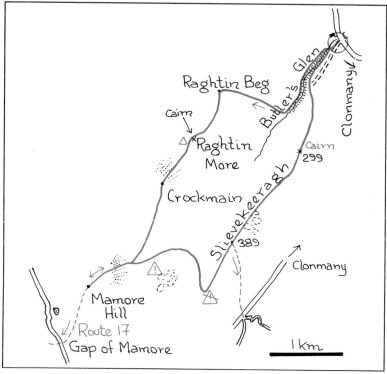

Route: Cross the wall just before the bridge; here at the start you must make the first decision: how to walk the length of Butler's Glen, which lies to the right. You can walk the intermittent path through the dense undergrowth in the defile bordering the stream or you can cross the stream as soon as you can, climb the opposite bank and walk along the high ground beside it. The bottom of the defile has certain attractions, especially if you want to experience jungle conditions without the bother of travelling to the Amazon Basin: ordinary mortals will cravenly walk on the edge of bogland on the far bank.

The defile is straight and deep for a kilometre or so, after which you should leave it and climb directly through wet country to Raghtin Beg (416m), and then with scarcely a drop to the summit of Raghtin More (502m, 1.75 hours), crowned by a huge cairn and a trig pillar (their positions are reversed on the 1:50 000 map).

Most of the hard work having been done, you can advance quickly past a long sinuous lake to climb or by-pass the occasional scree slope on the way to Crockmain (460m, over 1400ft). The next target is Mamore Hill. To get there, drop fairly steeply from Crockmain into boggy country scarred by corrugations of turf workings, picking a line to the left of the direct one to cross two rocky hillocks. This will take you to the foot of a path which climbs the steep ground ahead and avoids the extensive scree which guards this approach to Mamore Hill.

Mamore Hill (423m, 2.75 hours) is highly attractive; it gives even better coastal and hill scenery than that enjoyed all the way from Raghtin Beg. Its top, consisting of a narrow, rocky ridge plunging southwards towards the Gap of Mamore, is the best in the entire area. It's well worthwhile to walk to the last of several cairns on the summit.

Retrace steps down the scree slopes to face a dull section facing Slievekeeragh. Here you have the choice of descending into a boggy valley to reach the top of the ridge south of the summit or attempting to contour around this valley to reach the same point, the latter route being marginally the easier. On the top of the spur, walk north to Slievekeeragh, and continue north to pass a fine square cairn on its northern top (299m). From here you can descend towards Butler's Glen again. There is a clear track some distance from its eastern side, but it is littered with rubbish and best avoided. Better by far then, to keep close to the bank and follow an intermittent path all the way back to the start.

Longer Variation: Descend south from the summit of Slievekeeragh to the road junction at GR 346432, here taking the track running east, the leftmost one (it initially looks like a driveway to a house) and then picking up route 15. You can follow this route all the way to Clonmany (and the bus) or Glen House (and the car). Walking time to Glen House is 6.5 hours (distance 18km, climb 1180m).

A to B Variation: To combine this route and route 17, walk south from Mamore Hill to the Gap of Mamore, taking care on the steep narrow spur. Veer left off the spur as you approach the road to meet a rough track, the start of route 17. The second car should be parked at about GR 298399. This point may be reached by driving from Fort Dunree (GR 2838), and forking left twice. The second fork, onto a narrow road, crosses a bridge and then climbs steeply. There are several places to park uphill beyond the bridge. Walking time is 4.5 hours (distance 10km, climb 1020m).

Route 17: THE URRIS HILLS

If one walk must be chosen in all Inishowen, this is it. A steep but short ascent from the Gap of Mamore leads to a high, narrow, rocky ridge, punctuated by abrupt declivities. Unfortunately the walk is all too short and the return along minor roads is pleasant but not spectacular — but don't forget that, with a second car, you can combine this route with route 16.

Getting There: Start around the top of the Gap of Mamore (GR 319430), where there are several places at which to park a few cars.

Walking Time: 2.75 hours (distance 9km, climb 480m).

Difficulties: It is a little difficult to navigate your way onto the top of the ridge which forms the upland section of the route, otherwise navigation is easy. Generally good underfoot conditions.

Map: 1:50 000 sheet 3 but half-inch sheet 1 will do.

Route: Walk the road to the south side of the Gap, here taking an encouragingly level track on the right — for a few metres. Sadly, you must leave it almost immediately to climb over rocks to the crest of the ridge to the west. Don't be misled by pt 365m to the north-west (not shown on the

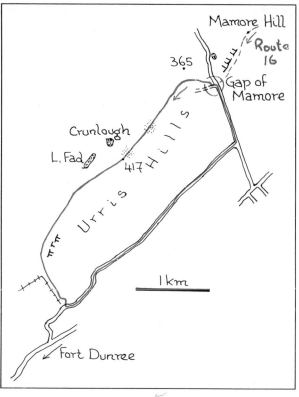

half-inch map). It's worth climbing for the view but it is not on the route. Once you attain the main ridge the way south-west is clear and the views all along here magnificent. A short section of high ground is followed by a couple of dips with short but steep scree climbs between. The second climb ends at the highest point in the Urris Hills, pt 417m/1379ft. If there are any lingering doubts about this point, the two scenic lakes, Crunlough and Fad, on the right of the ridge should dispel them.

From this point follow the high ground in a gentle leftward arc, steep slopes close on the left. Though it isn't critical, you might meet a fence paralleled by boundary stones running roughly south-east as you descend; this you can follow to the road (1.5 hours). Turn left here walk steadily gently uphill through remote country for over 3km, turn left at the tee and walk steeply uphill to the start.

Note

Fort Dunree (GR 2838) is near the end of the mountain section of the walk. It was a military fort from the eighteenth century and is now a military museum, with artillery pieces, weapons, maps and other records. It is worth a visit while you are in the area.

Route 18: SLIEVE SNAGHT (INISHOWEN)

Slieve Snaght at 615m is the highest point in Inishowen but as it is surrounded by stupendous areas of gently shelving bogland, not the most memorable. A long haul during which the panorama first reluctantly, but finally triumphantly reveals itself, ends on an outlier of Slieve Snaght. From here to the descent from another outlier of Slieve Snaght there are good views, though the terrain is nearly always wet and nowhere more than gently rounded.

Getting There: Park in the village of Drumfree (Drumfries on the signposts) (GR 3839), about 5 miles (9km) north of Buncrana on the R238. Swilly Bus run a limited service to the village.

Walking Time: 4.25 hours (distance 12km, climb 700m).

Difficulties: Lots of high vegetation and wet ground. Navigation generally easy, though the climb to Slieve Main over featureless, gently-sloped terrain may cause misgivings.

Map: 1:50 000 sheet 3 but half-inch sheet 1 will do.

Route: Take the R244 (Carndonagh road) for 50m or so, turn right onto a track and walk it for about 500m. At this point the track swings sharply right, and there is a farmyard on this side. Walk a few more metres and you will be confronted by a wide stream on the left, with a gate on the near and further bank. Here you should cross the river. (Only if the river is exceptionally high do you face the prospect of wet feet.)

Once across, a compass bearing of 123 degrees directly to Slieve Main is essential to navigate the gentle rises swelling ahead. Apart from high vegetation, and one fence which should be carefully negotiated, there is nothing to impede progress and also nothing much of interest except the gradually

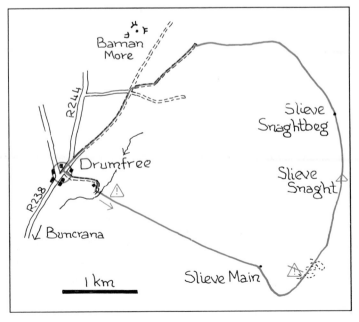

unfolding land- and sea-scape.

The summit of Slieve Main (514m, 1.75 hours) is a virtual plateau, with patches of boulder field here and there and a few small cairns, any of which could mark the highest point. The wide panorama, unbroken except in the direction of Slieve Snaght to the north-east, is some reward for efforts so far.

We must now turn our attention to this mountain. In good weather (don't chance it in bad), walk about 500m south-east to a bulge of Slieve Main's summit and from there head directly to the peat hags in the col facing Slieve Snaght (in bad weather simply head directly for the col). From the col climb directly and quite steeply to the summit, heralded by an area of rock slabs, most lying horizontally, but with the odd vertical one, thus giving the impression, in cloudy conditions anyway, of a particularly gloomy graveyard.

Slieve Snaght (615m, 2.75 hours) has a circular stone shelter surrounding its trig pillar, which therefore cannot be seen from any distance. As befits the highest point in all Inishowen, the views are wide. As well as most of the mountains of Donegal, Rathlin Island and some of the Hebrides and the Paps of Jura can be seen in good weather.

The descent is directly north over Slieve Snaghtbeg. On this descent make sure not to mistake a subsidiary cairn on a slight rise for the cairn on the summit, some distance off. From this summit head initially north-west over broken, boggy terrain, keeping as far as feasible to the higher (and therefore somewhat drier) ground. As you descend veer left towards the craggy face of Barnan More. This slow and erratic descent should eventually end on a bog track.

Before you head for the start, you might like to consider a short extension of the walk to Barnan More. Its steep-sided flanks of shattered rock are a sharp contrast to the bogland hereabouts and it overlooks a lovely area to its north. From its summit you can easily find your way back further south along the bog track you are now on.

If you decide on a direct return, turn left onto the bog track, and if it is the bog track that I think you should be on, turn left where this track meets another, and continue straight ahead (that is, do not take the one option to the right). This track will take you directly to Drumfree.

Route 19: THE NORTHERN CLIFFS

Of the several stretches of coastal cliff in Inishowen this is probably the longest, though there are others which are shorter but just as spectacular. With offshore islands, sea stacks and low but impressive cliffs to start and much higher cliffs, though without the seaward interest to end, this is a varied walk. Dull bogs landward make it impossible to form an attractive looped walk so you must do a part way there-and-back or have transport waiting at the end.

Getting There: Park at the 'Wee House of Malin' (GR 433582) (1) off the R242. To get there take the R242 from Malin village for about 6 miles (10km), turning right off it at Mullin's shop. Continue straight ahead to the seashore, where there is ample parking.

Return transport (car or bike) should be left at Glengad about 7 miles (12km) away. From the 'Wee House' follow the signs to Glengad and turn left at the sign 'Malin Head 14km' in the sprawling village of Glentooskert. Take the second turn left (it's after only a few hundred metres) and park at any convenient place before the road deteriorates too much (at about GR 515545).

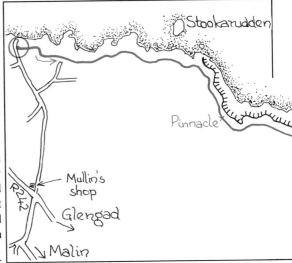

Walking Time: 3.5 hours (distance 10km, climb 360m).

Difficulties: Some rough ground but otherwise easy. No navigational difficulties.

Map: A map is really only useful to find the start and end of the route. 1:50 000 sheet 3 covers the entire route but half-inch sheet 1 covers only the western two-thirds.

Route: The start should be followed exactly; otherwise you might come to grief, as we shall see.

Walk eastward along the impressively wild storm beach and near its end after a few hundred metres, climb a narrow gully. At its end turn left to clamber out of it. You will now see that any other route would lead across fences or through a ploughed field.

A few fences still lie ahead and you should keep to the seaward side of them as best you can. Beyond them you can concentrate on the powerful coastal scenery: the Garvan Isles riding close in, Inishtrahull (the northernmost point of Irish land) beyond and an increasingly dramatic line of sea-cliffs, with two sea arches off shore. Also ahead looms the imposing cliff-bound, partly lichen-covered island of Stookaruddan. The cliffs rise for about 1km beyond Stookaruddan, reaching their highest point in this section at a phallic-like and easily recognisable pinnacle (1.25 hours). The grassy land beside this pinnacle is the recommended turning point if you intend to do a there-and-back walk. It is a marvellous eyrie, with a wealth of sea, mountain and coastline scenery to behold, including glimpses on the far horizon of the Scottish island of Islay and the Paps of Jura over 100km away.

If you are on the one-way route, walk downhill from the pinnacle to reach an area where there are bog cuttings and snatches of bog track, which may be of some help in a soggy area. Cross a stream and then climb along the left flank of Black Hill to reach another stretch of high cliffs falling in steep grassy slopes to the pounding sea. Quite impressive, but lacking the variety of

44

the earlier stretch.

After about 2km from Black Hill a small gully will cause a short detour inland and virtually force you onto a bog track. You can follow it all the way down to the waiting transport, but unfortunately it has been used as a linear rubbish dump by careless louts, so it might be better for sensitive souls to

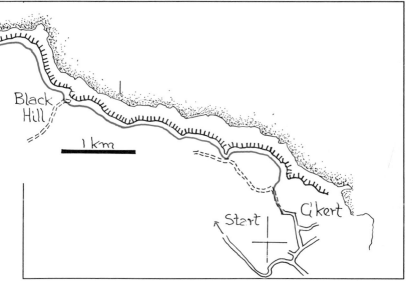

keep to the cliffs for another kilometre or so and then head directly inland to meet the bog track further down. Your transport should be somewhere down-hill on this track or its extension as a rough road.

Note
(1) The 'Wee House of Malin' seems to refer to the unimpressive cave, not the tiny church ruin. It is said that no matter how many people squeezed into the cave there was always room for one more, an attribute it shared with some present day hostels.

Directly north of Donegal town are the Blue Stacks, much of which rise above 600m and whose highest point is 674m. The core of this mountain range is the area round Lough Belshade, which is also a good reference point in an area which presents lots of navigational difficulties (routes 24, 25). Further west are the two Lavaghs (route 26) and to the east, abutting the dramatic, but all too traffic-laden Barnesmore Gap, are outliers of the Blue Stacks proper (routes 20, 23).

This whole area is remote, unforested and bears few marks of the hand of man. In addition the area round Lough Belshade is rocky and hummocky, with many relicts of the ice ages in the form of erratics, shattered boulders and tiny lochans sheltering among ice-smoothed slabs.

The arc of low hills to the north of the Blue Stacks is not so interesting, but beyond it we will also consider Aghla Mountain (routes 21, 22), just to the south of hill-bound Lough Finn, which shares some of the characteristics of the best of the Blue Stacks.

Route 20: BANAGHER HILL

An easy walk onto the virtual plateau of Banagher Hill (392m), where the numerous lakes form a pleasant foreground to the views of the nearby Blue Stacks and Lough Eske.

Getting There: If you can get to the start without error you can be more than confident that you will make no error on the route itself! The start is about 5 miles (8km) from Donegal town. From the town take the N56, turning right just outside it at the sign 'Letterbarrow 4'. Drive to the first crossroads, turn right and immediately left. At the tee 1.8 miles (2.9km) further on, turn left. Drive for a further 2.4 miles (3.9km) to a forestry entrance on the right (at GR 928859), where there is parking for several cars.

You can use a bike to get to the start; they may be hired in Donegal town. A more convenient starting point, particularly suitable for bikes, is given below.

Walking Time: 2.5 hours (distance 8km, climb 250m).

Difficulties: Some rough ground and one over-grown firebreak, otherwise no terrain or navigational difficulties.

Map: 1:50 000 sheet 11 or half-inch sheet 3, either of which might prove more useful on the car or bike journey than on the route itself.

Route: Take the track into the forest, shortly cross a tiny bridge and about 100m beyond it leave the track to cross disturbed ground on the right (the 1:50 000 map shows this as a track — it isn't). Keeping the major stream you have just crossed on the right, ford a minor stream and continue onward to the south-east along a narrow, positively claustrophic firebreak.

Though it is less than a kilometre long, this firebreak appears to last for ever, so the open ground ahead will be very welcome. Keeping forest close on the left round one right-angle bend and then strike out boldly for Lough Cam to

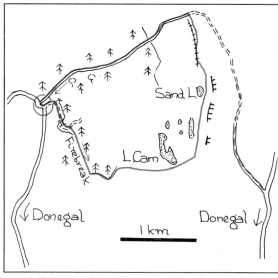

the east, passing on the way some spherical boulders bulging with stony warts, pustules and pimples — not a pretty sight.

From Lough Cam you can wander at will on the lake-studded plateau that is Banagher Hill, so the following is only one of several possible routes.

Walk east to the edge of steep ground overlooking Lough Eske and then turn north to pass Lough Fad and Sand Lough. Descend north, keeping a fence on the left to reach the road. On this descent the contrast between the rocky (right) and grassy Blue Stacks (left) is most striking. On the road turn left and walk through quite a variety of wood and field, punctuated by the occasional lonely homestead which seems to have almost succumbed to the forestry around it. At the main road turn left for the nearby start.

Alternative Start: The easiest way to reach Banagher Hill is from the east. Though this option does not give as attractive a route it does mean an easy journey of only 5 miles (8km) to the start from Donegal which might faciliate bikes. Take the road along the west side of Lough Eske, pass the entrance to Lough Eske Wood on the left and park at the next turn on this side (at GR 958847). From here you can easily climb to the plateau.

Route 21: LOUGH FINN

An easy walk along track and side road with attractive views of Lough Finn (1) and remote upland fields fronting rugged hillsides.

Getting There: The start (at GR 890006) is just off the R250 about 2½ miles (4km) south-west of Fintown, or 7 miles (11km) north-east of Glenties. From Fintown drive the length of Lough Finn and take the first turn left shortly after it. Park on nearby waste ground. From Glenties take the R250, watching out for the junction where the R250 swings sharply right and take the next turn on the right.

McGeehan's (phone 075-46150) runs a regular bus service to the area which might be useful if you are based in the south-west of the county.

You can park in several places along the R250 opposite Lough Finn. The only point about parking where suggested is that you may be lucky enough to have a kind non-walking driver who will pick you up at the junction where you emerge back onto the R250 and so avoid the comparatively dull stretch

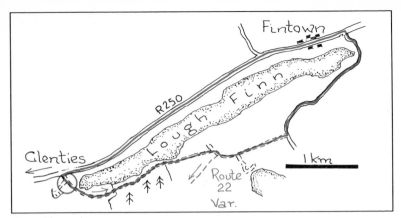

along this road.

Walking Time: 2.75 hours (distance 10km, climb 160m). If you do not walk along the R250 this reduces to 1.75 hours.

Difficulties: Some muddy patches, otherwise easy track and road.

Map: 1:50 000 sheet 11 or half-inch sheet 3 though neither really necessary.

Route: Take the track along the shore of Lough Finn (not the branch running south that ends at the disused quarry), and pass through two gates, the second of which leads into forest. The forest is dense and a little forbidding so it might be with some relief that you emerge into open country. Here the scenery towards Lough Finn and the hilly, grassy country ahead is excellent.

Take the track through a narrow gap, and ignoring the side road down to Lough Muck, continue uphill to a side road. Turn left onto it, take it over the shoulder of Scraigs, whose northern side falls towards Lough Finn in rocky cliffs. Assuming no pick-up on the R250, there is nothing for it but to walk the 4.5km back to the start. It carries some traffic of course, but the views it gives over Lough Finn and Aghla Mountain beyond are some consolation.

Note

(1) The name 'Finn' is reputed to derive from the girl Finna who was reputedly drowned in this lake while attempting to save her brother from being savaged, rather prosaically, by an angry pig.

Route 22: AGHLA MOUNTAIN

In an area of dreary, gently sloping soggy mounds, Aghla Mountain (593m), with its rocky escarpments, deep gullies and tiny knolls of shattered boulders, offers excellent variety and good underfoot conditions to the summit. From about halfway however the underfoot condition are much more bland, softer and wetter.

Getting There: The start is at the same point as route 21.

Walking Time: 3.25 hours (distance 9km, climb 530m).

Difficulties: Some wet, boggy ground on the second half of the route. Navigation is moderately difficult in parts, but with no cliffs in the area errors should not be serious.

Map: 1:50 000 sheet 11 is far preferable to half-inch sheet 3 in bad visibility

48

as it gives a much better idea of the shapes of the highland lakes, which might be an important navigational point under these conditions.

Route: Take the track along the shore of Lough Finn (that is, not the one that runs south to end shortly in disused gravel workings), pass through a gate and beyond it, at about the first house on the left, you will see two deep gullies on the right.

You can climb directly from anywhere around here, in or beside the gullies, but perhaps it is better to climb along the farther one as this gives a better approach to the summit. Above the gullies is a varied landscape of tiny peaks and hollows, eroded fragments of quartzite rock and tiny and not so tiny lochans. These latter are shown scattered in profusion on the 1:50 000 map, and as said above, are useful landmarks in an otherwise fairly confusing area.

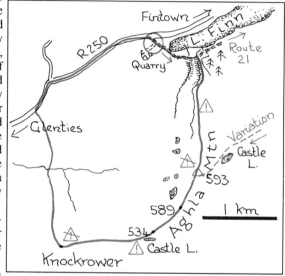

The best landmark of all however is provided by the Ordnance Survey: the trig pillar on Aghla Mountain (593m, 1.5 hours), though they are too modest to specify the relevant symbol on the map. The view from here is particularly fine: the rumpled mounds of the Blue Stacks away to the south-east and the more striking peaks of the Highlands to the north, with Slieve Snaght particularly prominent. Continue over high ground south to pt 589m and then swing south-west over pt 534m, south of which is Castle Lough (don't confuse it with the larger Castle Lough to the north-east). Rather disappointingly, the descent from here is into a tamer terrain of soft, wet ground. At Lough Analtmore, walk west to Knockrawer (457m), a rather undistinguished mound topped by a well-built cairn on a heathery plain.

Walk north from Knockrawer to reach the deep-set Sruhanacrow More River. From here there are several ways of getting back to the start, none of them particularly palatable. The simplest and recommended route is to head directly for the R250, watching out for fences on the way, turn right onto it and walk about 2km back to the start (the tempting route along the line of the dismantled railway is not feasible because of numerous fences across it). Alternatively you could head directly across moorland to the start, which you are unlikely to find enjoyable unless you are an enthusiastic bog trotter.

A Longer Variation: Take route 21 to the pass between Lough Finn and Lough Muck. Here head south-west, walking along the high ground to the south-east of the higher of the two lines of steep, rocky ground running from near the pass. Pass Castle Lough on the way to the summit of Aghla Mountain. The remainder of the route is as above. Walking time is 4.75 hours (distance 15km, climb 530m).

49

Route 23: BARNESMORE GAP MOUNTAINS

The deep, narrow glacial valley of Barnesmore Gap is bounded on the north-west by mountains which share to some extent the rocky hummocky country of the heart of the Blue Stacks. This walk traverses some of these mountains and returns through the Gap along the dismantled railway track.

Getting There: The start is at the forestry entrance on the N15 at GR 043875. From Donegal town, which is 9 miles (14km) away, take the N15 through Barnesmore Gap, then watch out for the prominent Barnes Bridge. The forestry entrance on the left is just beyond it. From the other direction, the best indication is the forest track on the right. Table 290 Bus Eireann service may be used for this route and is essential for the A to B variation.

If you are travelling by bike from Donegal, start at Biddy's O Barnes, the prominent pub on the left as you enter Barnesmore Gap, thus reducing the bike trip to about 7 miles (11km) each way.

Walking Time: 5 hours (distance 14km, climb 860m), though the walk can easily be shortened by walking out past Barnes Lough as described below.

Difficulties: Some wet terrain in the lower ground, otherwise good. Navigation fairly easy except in some featureless country around Croaghnageer. With few cliffs in the area, mistakes should not be too serious, though take care on the section from Croaghconnellagh.

Map: 1:50 000 sheet 11, though half-inch sheet 3 might do.

Route: Walk the track from the forestry entrance for about 1km and where it turns sharply right, leave it to cross the stream ahead and climb directly through an increasingly bouldery terrain to Brown's Hill (498m, over 1600ft), passing on the way its cairned south-eastern top.

From here cross the boggy col to the west and after that you can wander at will, maybe taking in all three indistinct peaks of Croaghnageer, which give excellent views of the nearby core Blue Stacks to the west. However perhaps the most elegant circuit is to take in pts 521m and 571m of the trio, crossing a north-south ditch on the way between the two (on the half-inch map these two tops are simply indicated by a 1700ft contour loop).

From pt 571m (2 hours) descend the rocky, rumpled spur running south and cross the lonely headwaters of the Barnes River about 1km upstream of Barnes Lough. Incidentally, on the 1:50 000 map this modest spur glories in the exotic name Tawnawully Mountains, its domain however sadly curtailed on this map compared with the half-inch.

You will have already noticed that Croaghconnellagh (523m) rises imposingly and unrelentingly ahead, and you've guessed it, this is the next target. (OK, it doesn't have to be — you can walk east to Barnes Lough and then pick up the outward track.) It's a straightforward but tough climb to the summit (4 hours) where there are a plethora of cairns on each of several worthy candidates for the highest point. (There is no trig pillar, though one is shown on the 1:50 000 map.)

There are cliffs and steep ground to the south and east of Croaghconnellagh, so you should descend south-west from the summit, keeping steep ground on the left until you reach Lough Nacroagh (just about shown on the half-inch map) or tiny Hugh Boyle's Lough. Here descend south towards the road (the N15 again of course), on which descent you will see a large building on the near side of the road with a carpark opposite it: Biddy's O Barnes. Aim for the left of both it and the highest house. This bearing should take you to an outhouse from where you can take a track to an abandoned section of the N15 (it's quite an interesting example of road construction of yesteryear). Turn left onto this and left again onto the

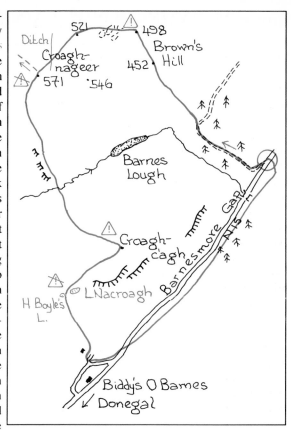

busy N15. Mercifully you need endure this for a few metres only, because at some waste ground on the right you can cross a bridge to the old railway track (1) clearly visible from the road.

The 3km of the rest of the route is along this track, and if you are lucky your stride will match the distance between the grass ridges left from the dismantled sleepers. After passing through a short section of forest, walk a few hundred metres more and then turn left to cross a stream and reach the N15 again, with the start close by.

A to B Variation: Walk to Croaghnageer as described under the main route, climb Croaghanirwore to the west and then descend west to the Ulster Way near the headwaters of the Corabber River. Take the Way south to the road along the western side of Lough Eske and walk 8km on country roads into Donegal town. Walking time is 6 hours (distance 20km, climb 630m).

Note

(1) The railway line running from Stranorlar to Donegal town was opened in 1882, the start of its construction having been hampered by seven weeks of snowstorm. The line closed in 1959.

Route 24: NORTHERN BLUE STACKS

The rocky hummocks which form the fascinating heart of the range can be reached from the north, though the car journey may be longer than that from the south. This route starts and ends with a walk over mostly wet boggy terrain, but the central section is an exhilarating traverse. This route can be easily lengthened at both ends of its high central section.

Getting There: Not easy. The start is about 13 rough miles (21km) east of Glenties and 13 not so rough miles west of Ballybofey. To get there from Glenties take the R253 (that's the road that passes the town's fire station) and keep to it for about 11 miles (18km). Turn right here (it's the first turn for miles) and park at the left turn after another 1.6 miles (2.6km) at GR 960942 (there is ample parking).

From Ballybofey take the R252, fork left onto the R253 (Glenties road) after 4 miles (7km) and take it for about 8 miles (13km), turning left here (the second in less than a mile). Park at the left turn after another 1.6 miles (2.6km).

Walking Time: 5.75 hours (distance 16km, climb 950m).

Difficulties: Good underfoot conditions except at the boggy start and end. Navigation is difficult over the high ground. If you are in trouble simply head north towards the road as there are only a few stretches of steep ground in this direction.

Map: In this area of hummocky peaks 1:50 000 sheet 11 is far preferable to half-inch sheet 3, though you may get away with it in good weather. In bad visibility the terrain may defeat any map, however good.

Route: Take the side road south, cross the bridge before the farm and the one to its right. Keep the fence on the right to ascend steadily southwards along the stream. After nearly 2km take the left fork where two tributaries meet and follow it for a while (the important fact to remember here is that you are going to climb Glascarns Hill on the east of the valley, so if you miss the junction it doesn't matter too much).

Eventually you must leave the safety line of the stream and strike out boldly through an increasingly rocky terrain for the summit of Glascarns (578m), crowned by an assemblage of massive boulders. Glascarns marks the start of the core Blue Stacks terrain to be enjoyed until the final descent: tough, predominantly rocky country with no definite peaks.

Turn south after Glascarns, cliffs on the left, to climb pt 641m (over 2000ft) (2 hours) whose only characteristic feature is Lough Aduff just to its east. Not much of a landmark, though considerably better than anything for the next few kilometres.

The next task is to find your way across the heart of the Blue Stacks, as I have said before a region with no definite peaks but with erratic rocks, huge slabs of granite and shattered boulders to contend with. Basically the task is to reach pt 674m/2219ft, about 3.5km away to the south-west. On the way you will climb pt 642m/2218ft and pt 626m at each end of a stretch of high ground, and then descend into lower ground before climbing pt 674m. There are two navigational aids on this long tricky stretch. One is the ubiquitous Lough Belshade, the other the huge white unmistakable (yes, really unmistakable) outcrop about 250m to the west of pt 626m. With these two good landmarks … you can still go wrong!

In spite of the symbol on the 1:50 000 map, there is no trig pillar on pt 674m (3.5 hours), the highest point in the entire Blue Stacks. Instead, at the

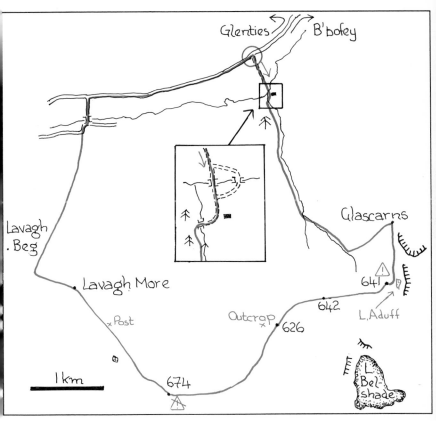

summit cairn you will find an OS metal cover, visible from a considerable distance — as long as you are directly above it.

This summit marks the transition from rocky to grassy terrain and the end of navigational difficulties. From pt 674m walk north-west to Sruell Gap, where there is a lone wooden post marking one route of the Ulster Way. From there it is a stiffish climb to Lavagh More (671m), which has two minor peaks barely rising above the summit plateau. Descend west to the high col facing Lavagh Beg, from where you can commence the trek into lower, wetter country to the north, the aim being to reach the bridge over the Reelan River (at GR 937933). Take care to avoid damaging fences on this descent.

Cross the bridge, turn right at the tee and walk the pleasant 2.5km to the start. On this stretch you can see the far-off white outcrop clearly if weather allows. Let's hope you could see it when you really needed to!

Route 25: SOUTHERN BLUE STACKS

This is the classic approach to the rocky, hummocky core of the Blue Stacks, starting at a point which leaves you within easy striking distance of Lough Belshade, a useful reference point if visibility is poor. If you intend to do only one walk in the Blue Stacks and are starting at the south of the range this is the route to choose.

Getting There: From Donegal town, which is about 7 miles (11km) away, take the road along the west side of Lough Eske, following the signs to Harvey's Point Country Hotel. When you reach the sign indicating that it is 1km away, keep straight ahead for 2.5 miles (4.0km) and turn left at an acute bend, where there is an Ulster Way waymark. Drive to a small parking place at the end of tarmac (GR 973870).

Bikes may be hired in Donegal town.

Walking Time: 4 hours (distance 10km, climb 570m), including some time for route finding.

Difficulties: As already said, a difficult area for navigation, so keep to the safe shores of Lough Belshade if visibility is bad or worsening. There are short, easily bypassed sections of rocky cliff towards the end of the unabridged walk.

Map: On all except the best days take 1:50 000 sheet 11. In poor visibility take half-inch sheet 3 only if you are pretty confident in your ability to navigate without a map or else tired of life.

Route: Take the track of the Ulster Way northwards, pass a forestry plantation on the right and, a short time after, climb a grassy ramp close to the hidden cascade of Doonan Waterfall East, thus eliminating a vee in the track. You now find yourself in a soggy river valley flanked by rocky hillsides, the Corabber River on the right, the Ulster Way underfoot, and with the track about to expire at a small hydro works (1).

About 15 minutes from these works you have to find a path heading off left to Lough Belshade. It's not difficult. First watch out for a waymark on a

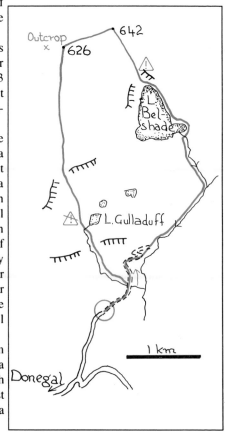

grassy hummock, then a stream flanked by a path which enters the Corabber River at right angles. Follow this path, of which it might be charitably said that it is no wetter than its surrounds, all the way north-west to the lake (1.25 hours) (2).

The lake is a gem, its shores sheltering tiny beaches of yellow sand in secluded coves, its sides guarded in parts by ramparts of granite cliff, behind which the high peaks of the Blue Stacks lie in an arc in all directions except the south-east. It is a good place to linger and maybe contemplate the next move.

In good weather at least you can wander where you like, so the following is just one suggestion among many. Use the rough dam to cross the outlet stream from the lake and walk along the north-east shore to a tiny beach at the northern end. From here you can climb steeply, a ravine close on the left and vertical slabs further away, directly into high rocky country and so reach pt 642m/2118ft. Continue along the high ground south-west to pt 626m (2.75hours) where, 250m or so to the west, is a large unmistakable white quartzite outcrop, the one and only beacon in the desert.

From pt 626m head almost south, aiming for the headwaters of a stream which empties into Lough Gulladuff. This is the most difficult part of the route, because there are two stretches of cliff, neither more than a few hundred metres long, overlooking Lough Gulladuff and its sister lakes from their west and north. They are easy to circumvent, but it is better to come down, steeply but on grass, by the stream between them.

When you reach Lough Gulladuff follow the outlet stream through the soggy swamp, interspersed with grassy hummocks, in which it lies. This will take you over a rocky line of ramparts through which the stream plunges in an impressive cascade. Beyond this cascade descend alongside the stream to turn right onto the initial track.

Short Variation: Just to remind you that a walk to Lough Belshade is easy, safe (but wet underfoot), and gives you much of the flavour of the Blue Stacks. The walking time is 1.25 hours to the lake and about an hour back.

Notes

(1) The hydro works, though an unwelcome intrusion in a remote and scenic area, are certainly not the worst of their kind.

(2) Monks fleeing from English troops in 1593 are reputed to have hidden their treasure on an island in Lough Belshade. No one knows which, but there are only a few tiny islands in the lake so it might be worth investigating.

Route 26: SRUELL GAP

Few routes in Donegal start at a point as difficult to reach as this one and few traverse such remote territory. The route crosses the edge of the plateau above the magnificent Grey Mare's Tail Waterfall, climbs to the grassy Lavaghs and then skirts the border of the central Blue Stacks, though it does reach its highest point (674m). It may be easily shortened by walking out at Sruell Gap.

Getting There: From Donegal town, which is about 8 miles (13km) away but seems longer, take the N56, turning right shortly at the sign 'Letterbarrow 4'. Continue straight ahead for 2.0 miles (3.2km), here taking the second of two closely spaced turns on the right. Continue to a tee, turn right and take a turn left after nearly 1 mile (1.5km). Park at the fork after 1.7 miles (2.7km) at GR 913880, where there is space for a few considerately parked cars. (The fork to the right is shown as a track on the 1:50 000 map: in fact the two roads are of equal quality, that is abysmal.)

Walking Time: 5 hours (distance 13km, climb 850m).

Difficulties: Lots of wet ground on the entire route and some difficult navigation after Sruell Gap.

Map: 1:50 000 sheet 11. Half-inch sheet 3 is not really good enough except in excellent weather.

Route: The start may be varied depending on your inclination, the inclination of the terrain you dare to climb, and the need to avoid private property. For what it's worth, I took the left fork (this start is common to all approaches), turned first right after about 700m, walked past a house and outhouse and then worked my way a trifle nervously upwards and leftwards through the rocky buttresses guarding the plateau to the north. Alternatively, you could keep to the initial road until you are about opposite Meenaguse Lough and make an easier approach from there.

Either way, once on the plateau, turn east to walk past Lough Anabrack and cross the stream which is preparing for its imminent headlong plunge as the Grey Mare's Tail Waterfall, which you won't see it until much later in the day. Then walk north to Lough Asgarha, a pretty lake enhanced with lots of reeds and, when I was last there, a landing place for noisy and ungainly ducks. From here the ascent to Lavagh Beg is easy: simply thread your way through a group of large and not particularly inspiring lakes and then climb the drier and rockier southern side of Lavagh Beg (650m, over 2000ft) (2.5 hours). Lavagh Beg has a few small lakes on its summit and a cairn on its northern side: the views are good to the north and west but much of the eastern aspect is blocked by Lavagh More, to which we must now pay attention.

Descend to the high col facing Lavagh More and then climb directly to the summit (671m), or rather two summits each with a cairn on a tiny common plateau. From here it is a rather disheartening drop to Sruell Gap, where there is a large post indicating that you are on one branch of the Ulster Way. Disheartening, because you must now regain all that descent and more on the way to pt 674m (2219ft) to the south-east. However, Sruell Gap (1) is a good drop-out point: you can simply head south-west through wet terrain for 3.5km to reach the start about 1 hour away.

The climb to pt 674m (3.75 hours) is another straightforward one. As noted elsewhere there is no trig pillar on the summit, in spite of the symbol on the 1:50 000 map. You are now on the verge of the rocky Blue Stacks so from here on rock will predominate on the left and grass on the right. Descend south-west over the indistinct pt 597m, keeping to the high ground and watch-

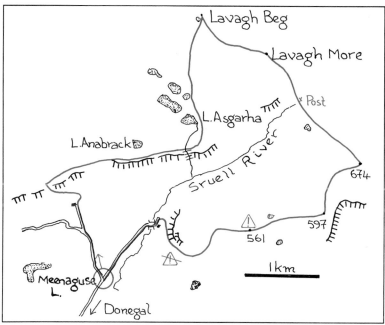

ing out warily for rocky cliffs on the left. Beyond it, swing west — and here the impressive Grey Mare's Tail Waterfall is seen across the valley for the first time — to walk over broken ground and pass pt 539m. Here a lake about 30m long may be some reassurance in an area with few distinct landmarks. (It is not on the 1:50 000 map though strangely, it appears to be shown on the half-inch.) From here climb the hill to the west, pt 561m (over 1800ft).

A little care is needed on the final descent. The idea is to use the bridge serving the last house on the south-east side of the valley. To get there you could head north-west from pt 561m and descend steep grassy slopes; this is the route suggested in bad visibility. Alternatively, and this is the good weather route, head due west from pt 561m and then swing left where the ground steepens, thus evading the rocky buttresses of the direct descent. Once under them swing back right and, to avoid disturbance, head to the right of the last house to reach the end of a track. Turn left, cross the bridge and walk the short distance to the start.

Note

(1) Sruell Gap used to be a route for pilgrims on their way to and from a pilgrimage place in north Donegal. The pilgrims were barefoot, not I suspect for any penitential reason, but because this was the only way to keep boots dry through the inevitably wet vegetation of the Gap.

The West, as the term is used here, covers the coastal strip from Bloody Foreland in the far north-west as far south (and including) the great bulge of land reaching westward in south-west Donegal, which we will call, in the absence of any consensus as to its name, the Rossaun peninsula.

With a highly indented, rocky coast and numerous off-shore islands, this is an area of sea-cliff and coastal walking, with the usual problem of making a satisfactory loop, especially since the inland areas may be uninteresting moorland. Of the sea-cliff areas the one which is best known, and rightly so, is Slieve League (route 30), at 595m the highest point in the entire area. Nonetheless there are other stretches of sea-cliff that are just as dramatic, though not as high (routes 29, 31, 33) and other coastal areas which offer gentler walking (routes 27, 28). Only in Rossaun is there much scope for good hill circuits (route 32, 34).

Route 27: ST JOHN'S POINT

The long narrow peninsula ending at St John's Point is worth a visit on a day of low cloud. This is a karstic area with outcrops of limestone which give it slight overtones of the Burren though on a tiny scale. Take any road south from Dunkineely (GR 7676) on the N56 and drive to the beach about 5 miles (8km) away. From here it is well worth while walking to the end of the peninsula (it's only a kilometre or so) or you can wander along the road in the other direction.

Route 28: CROAGHEHLY

The small-scale but rugged hills east of Crohy Head consist of low flat rocky ridges rising to only 245m, with steep scree-strewn sides. Definitely an area where you can wander round without any fixed plan so that the following suggestion is only a framework for further exploration.

Getting There: From Dunglow (about 4 miles (6km) away) follow the signs for Maghery and park in the village (GR 7108).

Walking Time: 2.75 hours (distance 9km, climb 320m).

Difficulties: Some wet ground. With a road never more than about a kilometre away there are no navigational problems that can't be easily solved.

Map: 1:50 000 sheet 1 is much better than half-inch sheet 1, though neither is really necessary if visibility is good.

Route: Continue onward from the village, passing the youth hostel. Ignore the fork on the right a few hundred metres on, and then watch out for a track coming in from the right. Take the track almost opposite, fork right after a few metres and continue upwards into mountain country to take the next track left, initially downhill. Fork right after a few metres. From here you can forget about directions for a while and concentrate on the scenery, rocky moun-

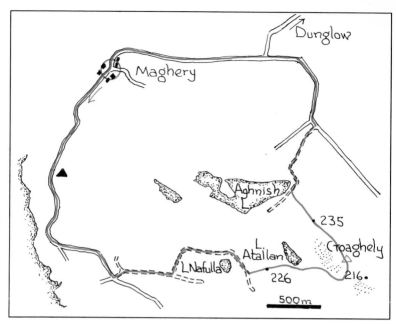

tain ahead and a wild sweep of ocean behind.

The track rises onto the plateau and passes a small lake on the right, Lough Nafulla, beyond which it peters out close to an indeterminate top, pt 226m. What is not indeterminate however is the summit of Croaghegly (245m) to the east, as the trig pillar on the top is clearly visible from here.

Descend steeply to the southern shore of Lough Atallan (barely depicted on the half-inch map) and from there tackle Croaghegly from the pass to its south-east, thus avoiding scree slopes guarding a direct approach. Walk along the hummocky ridge north-westward towards Aghnish Lough and turn right onto the track running along its near shore. From here it is easy to reach tarmac (unless you try to square the road system in view with the 1:50 000 map — the map is incorrect). Turn left onto tarmac to reach Maghery.

Variations: The 1:50 000 map will readily suggest other routes in this area. For instance you could walk further along the road to pass the two viewing points and then walk north-west along the entire ridge of which Croaghegly is the highest point. Or you could visit the lakes in the valley south-west of the Croaghegly ridge, or walk by road around the entire group of hills.

Route 29: ARAN ISLAND

The ferry to Aran Island (also called Arranmore), which threads through tiny islands and narrow channels, is a scenic treat in itself. Though the highest point of the island rises only to 227m there is marvellous sea-cliff scenery on the deserted north and west coasts, particularly around Torneady Point. The bogland and the higher points rising above it are also worth leisurely exploration.

Getting There: By ferry from Burtonport (GR 7115). The journey takes about 20 minutes. Check times beforehand as the service in summer (about every 90 minutes or two hours) is not all that frequent. You can leave your car near the pier in Burtonport.

Walking Time: 4.5 hours (distance 15km, climb 410m).

Difficulties: None, except for some boggy land around the central hills.

Map: 1:50 000 sheet 1 is preferable to half-inch sheet 1 as it gives a much better idea of the bog tracks and the summits, though the half-inch sheet will suffice in this, a safe area for walking.

Route: There are two piers at Leabgarrow, the biggest settlement on the island, but whichever you happen to land on, walk inland looking out for Glen Hotel. Keep it on the right and head uphill. At a tee (you are still in the

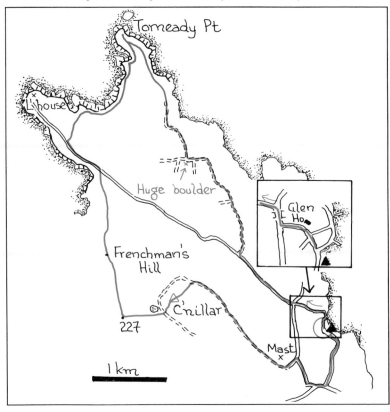

village), turn right, cross a bridge immediately and turn left. From here on plain sailing for a while.

After less than 15 minutes walking steadily uphill, turn right down the first track (it bends shortly left into a more encouraging direction) and continue on it until it swings left (west) in bogland. Then take the first right turn off it — it's at a huge boulder. (An aside: on my visit in the summer of 1994 I was appalled by the dumping along the bog tracks here and elsewhere on the island. Even by average none too exalted Irish standards it was bad. I hope something has been done about this by the time you visit.) Follow this track to its end and continue onward, north-west over a carpet of short grass, to reach Torneady Point (1.5 hours), a truly wonderful standpoint 120m above an ocean fringed with tiny islands and sea stacks. From here follow the cliffs south and then west, a stretch of constantly changing sea-cliff delights, to the road, within a few hundred metres of the lighthouse.

When you reach this road and study the map several routes will suggest themselves. The following makes no claims to be the best, though it does take in the highest point on the island, and so gives correspondingly wide views.

Walk south to climb Frenchman's Hill, which is visible from the lighthouse road, and then cross a complex pattern of bog tracks to reach pt 227m to the south. From here, as well as a fine array of coast and mainland mountain, the next target may be seen. This is the trig pillar on Cluidanillar (226m/750ft), reached over more bogland. Walk north-east from Cluidanillar to pick up a bog track running south-east and take it past a communications mast. Just beyond it turn right steeply downhill and so reach the main road. Swing left shortly with this road, thus ignoring the sign right for Pally's Bar. (It might be important not to make a mistake here if your ferry is due to leave.) This road will take you without further deviousness back to the south pier.

Route 30: SLIEVE LEAGUE

The sea-cliffs of Slieve League (595m)(1) are renowned, partly (I am guessing) because it is possible to view the entire stretch of mighty cliff without walking more than a few feet from your car. The highest point of this line of cliffs is at the summit of Slieve League and the walk there is an easy one. You can of course return by the same route but that described here takes an inland alternative.

Getting There: The start is about 14 miles (23km) west of Killybegs. From the town take the R263 to Carrick, turn left in the village, and right at the sign 'Bunglas/The Cliffs' near the post office in Teelin. Continue to the end of the road at GR 558757, passing through a gate on the way. Take it easy: on some steep gradients the bonnet of the car is the only object visible ahead and the road is probably heading off mischievously sharply right or left.

Walking Time: 4.75 hours (distance 13km, climb 770m).

Difficulties: None, except for the mildest of vertigo on the so-called 'One

Man's Pass'. Navigation easy and underfoot conditions good.

Map: 1:50 000 sheet 10, but half-inch sheet 3 is adequate.

Route: If you have a cliff on one side and a path under your feet, as you have on Slieve League, there is little point in describing the route in pernickety detail. Simply take the path upward from the parking place and follow it. At one place (pt 435m on the 1:50 000 map) you can, if you wish keep to the rocky crest of the ridge, but if you don't fancy that keep to the perfectly safe path winding round to its right.

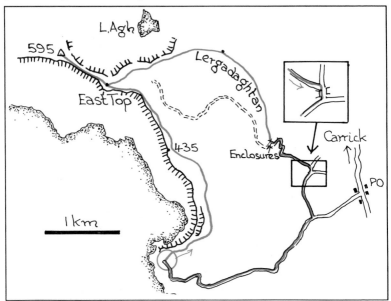

At length you will reach the eastern summit of Slieve League (over 570m, 1800ft) marked by numerous cairns on a plateau of soft ground, with similar ground (it's your return route, if you choose it) reaching away eastward. But for now the route is westward over the aforementioned 'One Man's Pass', which is simply a narrow level path with steep grassy slopes on both sides. Past this is the goal of the route, the trig pillar on Slieve League (595m, 2.25 hours). This is a marvellous viewing point with Ben Bulbin to the southeast, the tiny but high Stacks of Broadhaven off the Mayo coast to the southwest and perhaps the cone of Errigal to be seen off to the north. It's worth walking a little further on to see the Chimneys, a group of high stacks on steep ground seaward.

And so to the return, which is different in character but nothing like as memorable as the outward route. Retrace steps over the 'One Man's Pass' and walk east, the corrie of Lough Agh on the left, passing the holy wells and oratory (2). Drop to a narrow pass to their east and then climb the broad shoulder of Lergadaghtan Mountain (459m) (shown simply as a spur on the half-inch map). From here continue south-east to meet, at a set of enclosures, the inland track up Slieve League, sometimes disparagingly called the 'Old Man's Pass' (3.75 hours).

From here it is road, but a varied one, all the way to the start. Walk down from the enclosures, turn right at the tee, immediately cross a bridge and where instinct tells you almost infallibly to turn left downhill, turn right uphill. This track leads to the road on which you drove. Turn right onto it for the carpark.

Notes

(1) These sea-cliffs are variously described as the highest in Ireland / British Isles / Europe (take your choice). In sober fact, the sea-cliffs of Croaghaun on Achill Island are higher, but the Slieve League cliffs are the more impressive.

(2) The unprepossessing remains consist of little more than a few cairns and the ruins of a house, associated with Saints Aedh mac Bric and Assicus. There used to be a pilgrimage to this place, last held in 1909.

Route 31: SLIEVETOOEY

Slievetooey (511m) is more a long section of mountainside than a single peak; a series of minor summits, some separated by cols, others by stretches of high rocky moorland. The whole assemblage faces northwards to a stretch of wild and remote coastline. This walk takes in Slievetooey on the outward stretch and returns on a difficult undulating route along the steep ground and cliffs of the seashore.

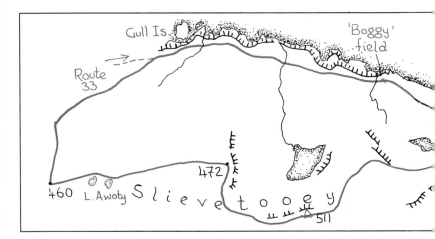

Getting There: The start is about 6 miles (10km) west of Ardara. Take the N56 from the town towards Killybegs, turning right shortly at the turn signed 'Maghera 5 3/4'. Continue for about that distance (in miles) to where the road swings sharply left inland and a sign on the right proclaims 'Caves 3/4' (1). Park here on waste ground at GR 661906.

Bikes can be hired in Ardara.

Walking Time: 6.25 hours (distance 16km, climb 890m) including some time for rough terrain.

Difficulties: The undulating rough ground and unexpected detours caused by changes in the direction of cliff edges, plus the three river crossings, make the end of the route tough going. If you suffer from severe vertigo think twice about doing the entire route as there are a few metres of mildly exposed climbing near the end. The good news: apart from all that the rest is easy, underfoot and navigationally.

Map: 1:50 000 sheet 10 though half-inch sheet 3 will do.

Route: Walk onward from the parking place for a few metres, pass the last house on the right and at the disused quarry just beyond it, follow the fence west and uphill. Beyond the fence continue uphill through rocky ground to pass Lough Acruppan (shown but not named on the half-inch map) on the right. Keep to the edge of the steep ground to the south-west of this lake and then swing left to climb over short grass to pt 511m/1692ft, which in spite of the absence of a symbol on the map, is crowned by a trig pillar (2 hours).

From this, the highest point on the route Slieve League to the south-west and Crownarad to the south-east rise over vast expanses of bogland and low hill. The unmistakable sea stack of Tormore Island, shaped like the top of a child's crayon, and the Signal Tower near Sturrall are prominent features to the west, while to the north the headlands, peninsulas and islands of the west coast of Donegal stretch to the horizon.

Drop to the sharp col to the west, after which climb steadily northwards to reach pt 472m (over 1400ft). The stretch to the west which follows is a pleasant one: good underfoot conditions with short grass and scattered rocks,

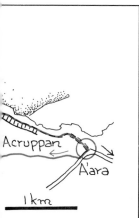

Acruppan

A'ara

1 km

little climbing and lovely views. In fact the only wet area is at the far end of the plateau at Lough Awoty where it and a sister lake are useful landmarks in an otherwise lakeless area. West of it there is a short climb to pt 460m/1515ft from where a long stretch of magnificent coastline to the west is visible.

From pt 460m continue north for about 1km and then north-east, all the time keeping to the highest ground. With this bearing you will eventually arrive opposite Gull Island (4.25 hours), joined to the mainland by a storm beach and a place of awe-inducing splendour. A good place for a stop.

While resting you might read again the paragraph under 'Difficulties' above, whose sentiments you might shortly come to share. The navigational objective from here on is simple: to keep the sea on the left, but it is difficult to give an exact route that can be readily followed. Do however note the streams you cross, the first of which just to the east of Gull Island; the third crossing is important for the end of the route.

So on a route of gradually tamer sea-cliff scenery, you will cross the third stream about 2.5km east of Gull Island. Just beyond it you will see what looks like a boggy field with cuts across it. Walk across this 'field' (it's actually a small area of bog) and beyond it keep to about the same level, watching out for a clear path which traverses the cliff ahead. Once on it stick to it. It crosses the cliff face and as already indicated has one moderately bad step. At this stage in the day and with little alternative but to go on, even the most fainthearted will doubtless persevere. The remainder of the route is obvious: keep between beach and sand dunes, still on the path, which you might now possibly share with the bucket and spade brigade. A nice gentle end to an adventurous day.

Note
(1) These caves are at the west end of Maghera Beach and can be visited at low tide.

Route 32: GLENGESH

Though not the most exciting area in Donegal, the fine glacial valley of Glengesh, its long grassy slopes here and there steepening into formidable cliffs, is a good walking area (see the photo on 1:50 000 sheet 10). You can do a simple circuit of the valley, but the route described here takes in a subsidiary valley and adds a touch of variety that the simple circuit lacks.

Getting There: Take the N56 from Ardara towards Killybegs. After about 1½ miles (2½km) turn right off it (signed 'Glencolumkille 25km'). Continue for a short distance to park near the school on the right (GR 722888). The route might also be walked using the table 298 Bus Eireann service. Alight at the junction 1km south of Common Bridge (at GR 727878) to avoid some of the road walk.

Bikes may be hired in Ardara.

Walking Time: 4.75 hours (distance 14km, climb 710m).

Difficulties: Much soft and some very soft ground underfoot. Navigation moderately easy in an area where no hidden dangers lurk, but take care in the featureless terrain after Common Mountain.

Map: 1:50 000 sheet 10 or half-inch sheet 3, the former of course preferable.

Route: Walk back down the road from the school, turn right onto the N56 and first right after about 1km. Walk steeply uphill until what has become a track passes within a few metres of a stream on the left. Ford the stream here. (You have now paid the penalty — in the form of a road walk — for the slightly more complex circuit.)

Once across the stream climb generally south keeping to the high ground. The first landmark is Lough Naweeloge, after which a fence will force you to swing right if the terrain doesn't. It's a steady and pleasant easy climb to Common Mountain (501m/1652ft, 1.75 hours), which has a trig pillar and of course commands good long views.

The descent is not so pleasant as the ground gets gradually boggier as you advance. Head about south-west along the high ground so that you eventually face Croaghnapeast. However, after 1.5km when you reach the col facing it, swing right so as to keep a forestry plantation on the right. Alongside the plantation the ground is really rough and rutted, so the road, when you hit it near its high point, will be welcome.

Cross the road and climb over boggy broken ground to Croaghavehy (372m), whose cairn lies at the far end of a plateau, but is worth while reaching because of the good views it gives to the west. From Croaghavehy turn north-east to pass by the side of an upland plantation and then commence the climb through rocky buttresses to Glengesh Hill. It is not worth while seeking its summit; instead walk north-east, parallel to the valley far below, through rocky ground enlivened by the occasional outcrop. Along here you can safely admire the cliffs across the valley which bound the south-east side of Glengesh.

When, after about 45 minutes from the plantation, the ground begins to slope downward ahead it is time to consider the route into the valley. Descend east, taking care to minimise fence crossing. If you aim slightly to the left of the road that crosses the valley you will probably find an easy descent route, but conditions may change, so you may have to use your initiative. Once on the main road in the valley, turn left for the nearby start.

An A to B Variation: With two cars you can combine this route and route 34 to give a satisfying north-south walk across the landward side of the Rossaun peninsula. The walking time is 6.5 hours (distance 17km, climb 1020m).

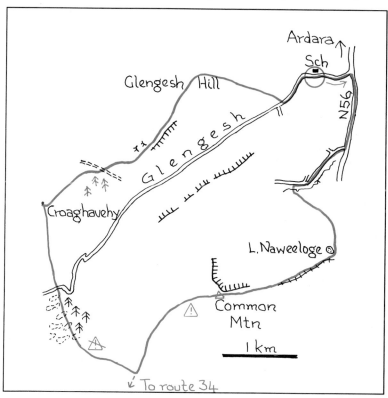

Leave one car at about the fork at GR 647769 (that is near the start of route 34). Start the walk at the side road near the start of route 32 at about GR 726878. Walk route 32 to the col near Crocknapeast, climb Crocknapeast and Balbane Hill (3 hours). Walk south-west (very wet in valley bottom!) to reach a forest track (this is near to where you leave the track in route 34 and the directions at this point under that route should be carefully followed), climb Croaghacullin and take route 34 to the second car.

Route 33: STURRALL

North of far-off Glencolumbkille (1) runs a line of sea-cliffs, remote, varied and as wild and demanding as any you are likely to meet on this coast. Unfortunately, it is bounded on its landward side by some dull moorland which is difficult to avoid unless you return by the same route. I have tried to pick out a varied return route but perhaps the outward one would satisfy most tastes.

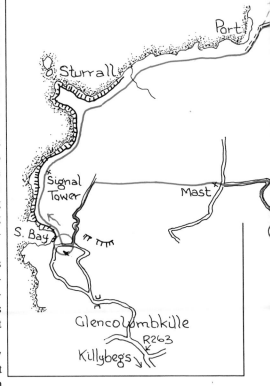

Getting There: Drive to Glencolumbkille. Turn left as you enter the village on the R263, take the first right (a gravel road), cross a bridge and turn left, and park under the high ground a little distance along (at GR 523859).

Walking Time: 5.5 hours (distance 17km, climb 630m), but this can be shortened to about 3.25 hours or less by walking only to Port and returning by the same route or directly, partly over moorland.

Difficulties: None as far as Port, then high ground plentifully sprinkled with navigationally useful lakes though with some soft underfoot conditions.

Map: No map is necessary as far as Port. After that 1:50 000 sheet 10 is much more useful than half-inch sheet 3. Note that the 1:50 000 map tends to be arbitrary in its use of contour lines on sea-cliffs.

Route: Climb the hillside around Skelpoonagh Bay directly from the start, keeping close to the sea-cliffs for the best views. Keep the Signal Tower (2) on the right and continue onward to the mighty sea-cliffs of Sturrall Head, which projects boldly westward into the ocean. It is possible to walk out along Sturrall Head — the initial path is on the north side of the headland — but unless you have a good head for heights do not attempt it.

Walk east from Sturrall along a gradually less imposing coastline: the eye is now drawn more to the off-shore islands further on, of which the great block of Tormore is the most evident. At the little stony beach of Port (1.75

hours) (the name is badly placed on the 1:50 000 map), you will have to decide what to do next. Specifically, whether to retrace your steps directly to the start or go on.

If you want to do the complete walk take the narrow road at Port into remote mountainous country and when past Kiltyfanned Lough climb south and then south-west into rumpled country nestling a whole flotilla of lakes. Any convenient route south-westward may be walked taking in for instance loughs Akeeran, Beg, White, Loughinisland (perversely the only one to have an island in the lough) and Astoller. West of Lough Astoller the country

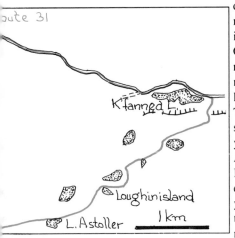

degenerates into dull moorland, relieved by excellent views down into the green oasis of Glencolumbkille. Walk to a nearby north-south track, take it to a radio mast, and continue west over trackless bogland towards the Signal Tower, picking up a track running south when near it. This will take you downhill to the start.

A Long Coastal A to B Variation: If you have a second car and an endless enthusiasm for sea-cliffs you can walk from Glencolumbkille to Maghera, using the start of this route and the end of route 31 and improvising the bit in the middle, which is covered in neither. At Gull Island you might consider climbing Slievetooey, so walking the start of route 31 in reverse. Walking time from Glencolumbkille to Maghera along the sea cliffs is 7 hours (distance 19km, climb 950m). The Bus Eireann service 296 (to Glencolumbkille) and 298 (from near Ardara) might also conceivably be used to facilitate this walk.

Notes

(1) There's a lot of interest around Glencolumbkille, including archaeological remains in abundance and a folk village, which can be seen on the initial climb.

(2) The Signal Tower was built during Napoleonic times when a French invasion was feared. Just beyond it, and before you reach Sturrall, you will see a beach far below where a ship went aground in the winter of 1870. Twenty-seven of the crew were drowned and only a few managed to scale the cliffs to safety.

Route 34: CROWNARAD

Crownarad is the highest point of a narrow ridge of north-south oriented mountains which dominates the N56 for a short distance west of Killybegs. The hills to the west of Crownarad are dull and forested, so that forest tracks in the valley directly to the west of Crownarad form a not altogether satisfactory lowland section of the route. Taking the easy variation shortens the forest walk.

Getting There: The start is about 7 miles (12km) west of Killybegs. Take the R263 from Killybegs towards Glencolumbkille, pass a viewing point on the left, drive for a further 2.1 miles (3.4km) and take the second of two closely spaced turns on the right — it's a narrow tarmac road. Fork left shortly and park at the forest entrance (GR 660783).

Walking Time: 4.5 hours (distance 14km, climb 580m).

Difficulties: Some wet underfoot conditions, otherwise good. Navigation easy, except on the featureless terrain south of Croaghacullin.

Map: 1:50 000 sheet 10, though half-inch sheet 3 will do. Sheet 10 shows some stretches of firebreak in the area as forest track.

Route: Take the track into forest and after about 15 minutes steady walking you should come to a gate on the right with an open area beyond and a rocky bluff beyond that. If you are short of time or simply hate a forest trudge you should climb by this bluff to reach the top of pt 381m (over 1200ft), thus considerably shortening the route. You can resume the commentary in the paragraph after next.

Otherwise, trudge on! Take the right fork at an old, tiny (really tiny) hut and after that cross two bridges, the latter taking you across the main stream in the valley. Now you should pay attention to navigation. About 5 minutes beyond the last bridge the track levels out; look out carefully for a wide firebreak starting a little way in on the right. Don't take it. Instead, plunge into the fairly scattered trees here at about 110 degrees compass, so heading for nearby higher ground. (It may be prudent to don waterproof clothing before you start to protect against moisture and pine needles.) The minor ordeal lasts about 5 minutes, after which you are on the lower, soggy slopes of Croaghacullin (1.5 hours).

Better terrain lies ahead. Climb Croaghacullin (394m/1327ft) and from there continue along the high, broken, featureless ground (you will probably have to resort to the compass). Climb pt 405m directly south and then swing south-west to climb pt 381m, where we rejoin the haters of forest trudges.

There is nothing much to distinguish pt 381m — like its predecessors it hasn't even a cairn — except for two features: a bog track ends to its east and more to the point, to the south a formidable rise to Crownarad begins as a grassy slope broken by peat hags.

The climb to the northern summit of Crownarad (493m, 3 hours) is straightforward, the rocky ridge reaching its characteristic narrow aspect as you ascend. In spite of the absence of a symbol on the 1:50 000 map this, the highest of the Crownard summits, has a trig pillar. The views are excellent: Slieve League prominent to the west; an expanse of coastline and peninsula to the south and the escarpment of Ben Bulbin across Donegal Bay. All of which and more to be enjoyed along the high ridge ahead.

The middle peak (over 460m) is topped by an ugly metal post, close to which is a simple, but poignant, typed message on a board giving details of the crash of a flying boat hereabouts in the Second World War (1). Continuing along the ridge, the southern peak (471m) is reached after a short rise. Because it gives a view unimpeded by the main ridge this top probably offers the best panorama of all.

The descent requires a little initiative. Continue down the ridge for about 1km, so walking parallel to a fence on the left. As you descend keep a watch rightwards for a suitable place to reach the road running along the south-east of the valley. On my explorations I reached it about 300m north-east of the fork in the road but it does depend on the day. Keep clear of sheep in fields and avoid proximity to houses.

Once on the road turn left, walk to the fork, turn right and walk to the start. Alas, the forest where you started is clearly visible at the end of a road seemingly stretching almost to infinity ahead. Think about that pint you are going to enjoy!

Note

(1) In March 1945 the flying boat, with a crew of 12, was on a routine mission from Lower Lough Erne in Northern Ireland to the nearer reaches of the Atlantic. All 12 were killed when the plane crashed near here. It was normal for allied planes to overfly neutral Ireland's air space, with the secret agreement of the Irish government.

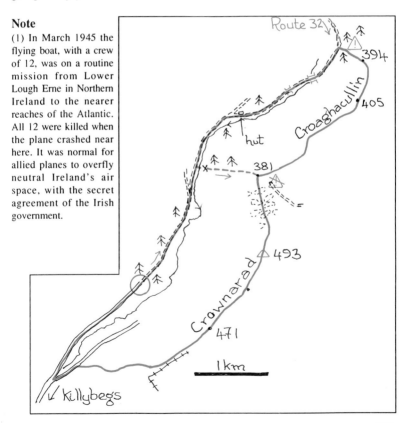

Appendix:
Useful Names and Addresses

- Glenveagh National Park, Church Hill, Co Donegal.
  Phone 074-37090.

- Bus Eireann, Bus Office, Letterkenny, Co. Donegal.
  Phone 074-21309.

- Swilly Bus Service, Head Office, Letterkenny, Co. Donegal.
  Phone 074-22400.

- North West Busways, Market Square, Moville, Co. Donegal.
  Phone 077-82619.

- An Oige/Irish YHA Head Office, 61 Mountjoy Street, Dublin 7.
  Phone 01-830 4555.

- Independent Hostels, Information Office, Glencolumbkille, Co
  Donegal. Phone 073-30130.

- Ordnance Survey Office, Phoenix Park, Dublin 8. Phone 01-820 6100.

- North West Tourism, Temple Street, Sligo. Phone 071-61201
  (There is a year-round tourist office in Letterkenny (phone 074-
  21160) and seasonal offices in Buncrana (phone 077-62600),
  Donegal Town (phone 073-21148) and Dunglow (phone 075-
  21297.)

- Malinmore Adventure Centre, Glencolumbkille, Co. Donegal.
  Phone 073-30123.

- Lough Gartan Adventure Centre, Church Hill, Letterkenny, Co.
  Donegal. Phone 074-37032/37092.